A Half Penny
on the
Federal Dollar

D1508851

A Half Penny on the Federal Dollar

The Future of Development Aid

Michael O'Hanlon
Carol Graham

Brookings Institution Press
Washington, D.C.

Copyright © 1997 by
THE BROOKINGS INSTITUTION
1775 Massachusetts Avenue, N.W.
Washington, D.C. 20036

All rights reserved

Library of Congress Cataloging-in-Publication data

O'Hanlon, Michael E.
    A half penny on the federal dollar : the future of
development aid / Michael O'Hanlon, Carol Graham.
        p.   cm.
    Includes bibliographical references and index.
    ISBN 0-8157-6445-6 (pbk. : alk. paper)
    1. Economic assistance, American—Developing
countries—Finance.   I. Title.
    HC60.O35   1997
    338.91'7301724—dc21   97-4697
                                                  CIP

9 8 7 6 5 4 3 2 1

The paper used in this publication meets the minimum requirements of the American National Standard for Information Sciences—Permanence of Paper for Printed Library Ma-
terials, ANSI Z39-48-1984.

Typeset in Palatino

Composition by Cynthia Stock
Silver Spring, Maryland

Printed by Kirby Lithographic Co.
Arlington, Virginia

₿ THE BROOKINGS INSTITUTION

The Brookings Institution is an independent organization devoted to nonpartisan research, education, and publication in economics, government, foreign policy, and the social sciences generally. Its principal purposes are to aid in the development of sound public policies and to promote public understanding of issues of national importance.

The Institution was founded on December 8, 1927, to merge the activities of the Institute for Government Research, founded in 1916, the Institute of Economics, founded in 1922, and the Robert Brookings Graduate School of Economics and Government, founded in 1924.

The Board of Trustees is responsible for the general administration of the Institution, while the immediate direction of the policies, program, and staff is vested in the President, assisted by an advisory committee of the officers and staff. The by-laws of the Institution state: "It is the function of the Trustees to make possible the conduct of scientific research, and publication, under the most favorable conditions, and to safeguard the independence of the research staff in the pursuit of their studies and in the publication of the results of such studies. It is not a part of their function to determine, control, or influence the conduct of particular investigations or the conclusions reached."

The President bears final responsibility for the decision to publish a manuscript as a Brookings book. In reaching his judgment on the competence, accuracy, and objectivity of each study, the President is advised by the director of the appropriate research program and weighs the views of a panel of expert outside readers who report to him in confidence on the quality of the work. Publication of a work signifies that it is deemed a competent treatment worthy of public consideration but does not imply endorsement of conclusions or recommendations.

The Institution maintains its position of neutrality on issues of public policy in order to safeguard the intellectual freedom of the staff. Hence interpretations or conclusions in Brookings publications should be understood to be solely those of the authors and should not be attributed to the Institution, to its trustees, officers, or other staff members, or to the organizations that support its research.

Board of Trustees

James A. Johnson
Chairman

Leonard Abramson
Michael H. Armacost
Elizabeth E. Bailey
Alan M. Dachs
Kenneth W. Dam
D. Ronald Daniel
Stephen Friedman
Henry Louis Gates Jr.
Vartan Gregorian

Bernadine Healy
F. Warren Hellman
Samuel Hellman
Robert A. Helman
Thomas W. Jones
Ann Dibble Jordan
Breene M. Kerr
Thomas G. Labrecque
Donald F. McHenry
Jessica Tuchman Mathews
David O. Maxwell
Constance Berry Newman

Maconda Brown O'Connor
Samuel Pisar
Rozanne L. Ridgway
Judith Rodin
Warren B. Rudman
Michael P. Schulhof
Robert H. Smith
Vincent J. Trosino
Stephen M. Wolf
John D. Zeglis
Ezra K. Zilkha

Honorary Trustees

Vincent M. Barnett Jr.
Rex J. Bates
Barton M. Biggs
Louis W. Cabot
Frank T. Cary
A. W. Clausen
John L. Clendenin
William T. Coleman Jr.
Lloyd N. Cutler
Bruce B. Dayton
Douglas Dillon
Charles W. Duncan Jr.
Walter Y. Elisha

Robert F. Erburu
Robert D. Haas
Teresa Heinz
Andrew Heiskell
Roy M. Huffington
Vernon E. Jordan Jr.
Nannerl O. Keohane
James T. Lynn
William McC. Martin Jr.
Robert S. McNamara
Mary Patterson McPherson
Arjay Miller
Donald S. Perkins

J. Woodward Redmond
Charles W. Robinson
James D. Robinson III
David Rockefeller Jr.
Howard D. Samuel
B. Francis Saul II
Ralph S. Saul
Henry B. Schacht
Robert Brookings Smith
Morris Tanenbaum
John C. Whitehead
James D. Wolfensohn

*To John Steinbruner
with admiration
and gratitude*

Foreword

*A*T THE END of the cold war, Americans understandably welcomed the opportunity to look inward after decades of intense strategic competition. Pressing problems on the home front and the rising costs of entitlements brought on by demographic change and improved medical technology demanded a greater share of the nation's treasure and attention.

These and other developments have had a dramatic effect on national security spending. Annual defense outlays will drop by more than $100 billion in constant 1997 dollars—or nearly one-third—over the course of the 1990s. By the turn of the century, the military will lay claim to less than 3 percent of the nation's GDP, down from roughly 6 percent in the 1980s. The trajectory of defense spending cuts, however, has begun to level, and the defense budget appears likely to stabilize at around $250 billion (in 1997 dollars), or roughly one-sixth of total federal outlays, by 2002.

The prospects for discretionary spending for international affairs, which totals $19.6 billion in 1997, are even gloomier. Under the president's budget projections from early 1996, it will decline by just as great a percentage as defense over the 1990–2002 period, against a much more modest base. No other major category of federal spending will undergo a real cut during this period. And unlike the defense budget, there is no evident floor under the international account. Indeed, the congressional budget resolution of 1996 and the president's recent budget request would reduce it substantially further.

Can these drastically reduced amounts of money do the job? It is to that question—and most notably the matter of assistance to developing countries, which accounts for almost half of all international spending— that Michael O'Hanlon and Carol Graham turn their attention in this Brookings study. Their analysis investigates what role we should assign to aid now that many developing countries have graduated from the category of aid recipients, other countries remain mired in poverty (despite having received large infusions of aid), and foreign investment flows to many developing countries are far greater than official development assistance.

The authors are grateful for the assistance of a number of individuals, especially Carol Adelman, Richard Blue, Barry Bosworth, David Dollar, Tom Donnelly, William Durch, Anthony Gambino, David Gordon, Kate Grant, Susan Hardesty, Twig Johnson, Robert Johnstone, Stacey Knobler, Sheila Murphy, William Myers, Lant Pritchett, James Schear, Sarah Sewall, Stephen Solarz, Nicolas van de Walle, Michael Van Dusen, Joe Whitehill, and numerous others from the State Department, United Nations, World Bank, Organization for Economic Cooperation and Development, and Agency for International Development. The authors especially thank Christina Larson and, in an earlier stage of the project, Sheila Roquitte for research assistance. They are also grateful to Richard Haass and John Steinbruner for guidance. Deborah Styles edited the manuscript, and Max Franke prepared the index.

Funding for this project was provided in part by The John D. and Catherine T. MacArthur Foundation and the Carnegie Corporation of New York. Their support is gratefully acknowledged.

The views expressed here are those of the authors alone and should not be ascribed to any of the aforementioned individuals or institutions or to the trustees, officers, or other staff members of the Brookings Institution.

MICHAEL H. ARMACOST
President

April 1997
Washington, D.C.

Contents

Figures

1

Introduction

A PROMINENT component of post–World War II foreign policy, U.S. development assistance has been extraordinarily effective. It has provided humanitarian relief and certain basic necessities such as child immunizations to impoverished peoples, promoted family planning services, helped produce the green revolution in global agriculture, and catalyzed general economic growth in a number of countries.

But in many other countries, aid has failed to stimulate broad-based and self-sustaining growth. The track record is particularly poor in situations where aid has continued to flow despite the recipients' continuance of harmful economic policies such as excessive consumer subsidies, overvalued exchange rates, oversized public sectors, large budget deficits, and significant trade barriers.

This mixed record leads to the conclusion that fundamental reforms are needed in U.S. bilateral aid programs as well as in the efforts of other donors and multilateral institutions. Subsequent chapters in this study describe U.S. and global aid efforts by region and by function; place them in broader economic, political, and historical context; evaluate their effectiveness; and spell out the budgetary implications of the new aid strategy that we propose.

What Is Development Aid?

This book addresses that part of U.S. international spending known as official development assistance (ODA). In 1997, the United States is spending about $9 billion on ODA.

Development aid constitutes the vast majority of all foreign assistance the United States and other donor countries provide to sub-Saharan Africa, South Asia, Central America, and poorer countries in other regions.

1

It includes the 40 percent of U.S. aid to the Middle East that is devoted to economic (as opposed to military) ends; it also encompasses assistance for purposes such as demobilizing soldiers in Central America and setting up better legal institutions in Rwanda. It does not, by the definition used in this study and by the Organization for Economic Cooperation and Development (OECD), include assistance to the former Soviet republics, former Yugoslav republics, or other countries in Europe. Nor does it encompass international broadcasting, as through the Voice of America.

In short, official development assistance attempts to promote human and economic advancement in the world's poorer countries. U.S. ODA is required, under the 1961 foreign assistance act as amended, to serve some thirty-three goals and seventy-five "priority areas."[1] But at some risk of oversimplification it can be viewed as serving four main purposes:

—humanitarian relief, such as that provided after natural or conflict-related disasters;

—grass-roots aid for activities such as provision of primary health-care services and support to certain types of microenterprises;

—general assistance for development of a national economy—focused on economic matters, but also directed to other national needs such as legal institutions; and

—targeted aid for purposes such as environmental preservation—protection of a wildlife refuge or substitution of an ozone-depleting chemical with a more benign substance in air conditioners, for example—or support for nongovernmental organizations or for election monitoring.

The motivations for giving these types of aid also range broadly. For example, aid for development may be given for primarily philanthropic purposes or partly for strategic reasons, as with economic support funds provided to the Middle East.

In this study, we group the first two categories together as aid that can and should be provided principally on moral grounds and largely independent of the policies of the recipient government. The third category accounts for most of the aid dollars provided by the United States and other donors and accordingly receives most of our attention. It is, in our view, more vulnerable to criticism and more in need of revamping. The last category has a much smaller dollar significance and is treated less thoroughly here.

ODA within the Federal Budget

ODA makes up almost half of all U.S. international discretionary spending (see table 1-1). Since international spending is just over one percent of the federal budget, ODA represents about one-half cent of every dollar spent by the U.S. government.

Total U.S. international discretionary spending totals about $19.6 billion in 1997. As shown in table 1-1, in addition to $9.2 billion for ODA that is analyzed in this study, roughly $6.4 billion a year is provided in other types of foreign aid. That includes military aid, chiefly to Israel and Egypt, of about $3.3 billion annually. It also includes programs that the Clinton administration calls "democracy building"—all types of assistance to the central European and former Soviet states and international broadcasting and exchange efforts ($2.4 billion annually). Finally, by our definition, it encompasses U.S. dues for United Nations peacekeeping operations and the bilateral International Military Education and Training (IMET) program.

The final $4 billion of international discretionary spending supports diplomatic activities, primarily in the State Department but also the U.S. share of various UN administrative costs, as well as efforts to promote U.S. business overseas through Export-Import Bank loans and related instruments.

The Prognosis for ODA

What will happen to ODA under various plans to balance the federal budget? The plans themselves do not say, but one can infer the likely fate of development assistance from their projections for the broader international account.

Current international discretionary spending of $19.6 billion, 15 percent below the $23 billion a year average of the 1980–95 period, would under the president's February 1997 proposal decline by another 15 percent in the future. The resulting spending level would total about $16.8 billion in 2002 (unless otherwise indicated, all budget figures in this study are expressed in constant 1997 dollars). International spending would drop as low as $13 billion under the Congress's budget resolution of mid-1996 (see figure 1-1 and figure 1-2). Because of the recent improvement in the deficit picture, however, a more realistic scenario given the 104th Congress's preferences might be an annual spending level of around $15 billion.

TABLE 1-1. *The U.S. International Discretionary Account*[a]
Billions of 1997 dollars

Type of spending	Estimated 1997 outlays	Total
Development aid		
Multilateral aid		
Development banks	1.7	1.7
Voluntary contributions to UNICEF, etc.	0.3	2.0
Bilateral aid		
Development assistance	2.3	4.3
Economic support funds	2.4	6.7
P.L. 480 food aid	1.1	7.8
Refugee assistance	0.9	8.7
Peace Corps, other	0.5	9.2
Other foreign assistance		
Aid to central/eastern Europe, former Soviet Union	1.2	10.4
Foreign military financing	3.3	13.7
International military education and training	0.05	13.8
Narcotics control	0.2	14.0
International Atomic Energy Agency, Korean reactor deal	0.1	14.1
U.S. Information Agency	1.2	15.3
UN peacekeeping	0.35	15.6
Bilateral and multilateral diplomacy		
State Department	2.5	18.1
Arms Control and Disarmament Agency, other	0.2	18.3
UN Secretariat, other UN organizations (administrative costs)	0.9	19.2
Business		
Export-Import Bank, other	0.4	19.6
Addendum: Aid funded out of the U.S. military budget		
Nunn-Lugar cooperative threat reduction aid for former USSR	0.4	
U.S. military costs in indirect support of UN peace operations[b]	1.5 to 3.5	

Source: Executive Office of the President, *Budget of the United States Government, Fiscal Year 1998* (February 1997), pp. 252–53.

a. The 150 account includes roughly $5 billion in negative spending (receipts from foreign governments and the like), so it totals about $15 billion in outlays in 1997.

b. It is impossible to estimate accurately the (mostly unreimbursed) U.S. military costs in support of UN peace operations in 1997. The estimate here reflects the 1994–96 annual average.

FIGURE 1-1. *U.S. International Spending, 1962–2002*[a]

Billions of constant 1997 dollars

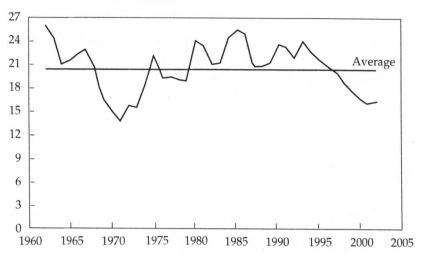

Source: Executive Office of the President, *Historical Tables: Budget of the United States Government for Fiscal Year 1997* (1996).

a. Data until 1996 are historical; figures from that point on are projections from the president's request for FY 1997. They are based on OMB's relatively optimistic economic assumptions of early 1996; a more pessimistic forecast would imply a need for deeper cuts somewhere in the federal budget, possible including international programs, to eliminate the deficit. Figures are outlays and use the definition of international discretionary spending from the Budget Enforcement Act, which includes funding for the State Department, UN peacekeeping, and other activities, as well as foreign aid. The president's 1998 budget request changes the curve only slightly; it would terminate at the slightly higher level of $16.8 billion if based on that more recent budget. The trough in the graph around 1970 is partly because, in that period, several billion dollars a year in military aid to Vietnam was routed through the defense budget rather than the international account.

What are the implications for ODA? Having averaged about $12 billion in the 1980s, and indeed over the entire 1960–95 period (see figure 1-3), today it is 25 percent below that earlier average. In other words, it has so far been cut more severely than other parts of the international budget.

ODA would drop to about $8 billion in 2002 under the president's official plan of February 1997. It could go as low as $6 billion under Congress's 1996 budget resolution. Given the popularity of Mideast aid, $2 billion of that remaining ODA amount might still go to economic aid

FIGURE 1-2. *U.S. International Spending, 1962–2002: Projections Based on the Congress's 1996 Budget Plan*[a]

Billions of constant 1997 dollars

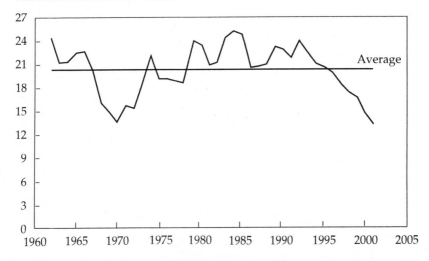

Source: Executive Office of the President, *Historical Tables: Budget of the United States Government for Fiscal Year 1997* (1996).

a. Data until 1996 are historical; figures from that point on are projections. Figures are outlays and use the definition of international discretionary spending from the Budget Enforcement Act, which includes funding for the State Department, UN peacekeeping, military aid, international broadcasting, and other activities, as well as foreign aid.

for Egypt and Israel—leaving about $4 billion to $5 billion for the rest of the world. Viewed from this perspective, the cut would be at least 50 percent relative to earlier decades.

Subsequent chapters of this study argue that, despite ODA's checkered past, such levels of assistance would be unacceptably low. Indeed, today's resources are already insufficient, though a return to the $12 billion level of the recent past would be adequate. Chapter 2 provides background on the history and current nature of development assistance; chapter 3 evaluates its effectiveness to date; and chapters 4 and 5 spell out a new strategy for future development aid as well as associated costs to the United States and the donor community as a whole. Chapter 6 summarizes our conclusions.

FIGURE 1-3. *U.S. Official Development Assistance, 1960–95*[a]

Billions of constant 1997 dollars

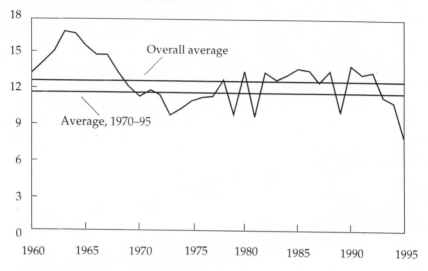

Sources: Organization for Economic Co-operation and Development, *Development Assistance Report* (Paris: OECD, 1996), pp. A9–A10; and DAC reports from previous years for earlier data. Also see Organization for Economic Co-operation and Development, "Financial Flows to Developing Countries in 1995: Sharp Decline in Official Aid; Private Flows Rise," Press Release (OECD, 1996).

a. In the U.S. federal budget, most ODA is found in budget function 151, which averaged $6.7 billion from 1971 to 1995 (in constant 1997 dollars). It remained $6.5 billion in 1997, but $1.2 billion of that amount was slated for nondeveloping countries (the former communist states). It will decline to $5.5 billion by 2002 under the president's budget, even as aid to former communist states remains $850 million.

Why Is This Subject Important?

Before embarking further on a detailed quantitative study of U.S. foreign assistance accounts, the subject should be put in broader perspective. What are U.S. interests in the developing world, and what is the role of foreign aid in advancing them?

It is difficult to determine how much the United States should care, in traditional national-interest terms, about the developing countries. Too often debates about this topic become polarized and ideological. Some argue that proliferating weapons, rapidly growing populations, and industrializing economies could pose serious environmental and security threats to the United States. Others assert that what happens in the world's poorer countries is of little direct concern to the United States. The United States trades heavily with only a few of them and rarely suffers when they engage in warfare. And in any case, the United States cannot easily influence those countries with economic aid.

While the current debates are inconclusive, the positions of both "globalists" and "realists" contain important elements of truth. U.S. interests in poorer countries are best thought of as significant and enduring, though generally not vital.[2] Several possible scenarios can be neither analytically established nor disproven: that the planet will not be able to feed itself next century; that it will not be able to adjust to possible large shifts in temperature and rainfall patterns; that it will not be able to contain civil conflict and terrorism.

This agnostic perspective argues in favor of some sustained attention to the problems and potential of poorer countries. It also justifies a certain expenditure of resources and sometimes the willingness to risk American lives—though how much and how often are clearly open to debate and are, in the end, matters of judgment as much as analysis.

We believe, however, that whatever its implications for traditional national interests, the way in which the United States addresses the developing countries does much to shape the overall character of its foreign policy. Remaining committed to helping other countries is critical for keeping many Americans engaged in foreign policy and for convincing other peoples around the world that this country still supports human rights, political freedoms, and economic opportunity for all.[3]

Such considerations should not be dismissed by those who consider themselves realists and are concerned only with matters of basic national interest. A moral element to foreign policy was quite important in the West's victory in the cold war. Countries were held together by shared values of democracy and freedom and reliance on market-oriented economic growth, as much as by military alliances, mutual economic self-interest, or diplomatic démarches.[4] Countries outside the western circle often were inspired by the vision offered by the United States, even when it was blemished by dubious policies in places such as Vietnam, Iran, Guatemala, and Zaire.

A strong, fair-minded, trade-oriented United States provided the type of "hegemonic stability" that many political theorists consider most conducive to a peaceful and prosperous international system. Even if the

United States was motivated to help others at least as much out of concern about stemming communism as philanthropy, its policies were helpful to most countries and were perceived to have a magnanimous element.[5]

If the United States is to invite countries to join it in a forward-looking and inclusive perspective on the future—and overcome the natural fears on the part of others such as China and Russia that it is simply pursuing global dominance at their expense—it needs to prove the sincerity of that outlook by making realistic efforts to help other countries when they need it.[6] The United States has a historic opportunity, as increasing numbers of countries throughout the world are turning to market-oriented and increasingly democratic approaches to economic and societal development.

What role does foreign aid have if markets and open politics are the answers to countries' problems? In many places, the answer is none or little. For example, most east Asian states and now many Latin American countries, are capable of attracting far more private capital and of collecting far more money in taxes to serve their own domestic needs than they could ever hope to obtain through official assistance. Many of the central European countries and former Soviet republics have the potential to be just as successful in these ways. For these countries, international trade and investment opportunities, together with stable international political conditions, matter much more than foreign aid. The United States does more to help them by reducing trade barriers, keeping its budget deficit down, and promoting international political stability through diplomacy and military deterrence than it could ever be expected to do through assistance programs.

But for many of the world's poorer countries, particularly in Africa, the Middle East, Central America, and the Caribbean, the picture is much different. Private capital flows and the availability of nonconcessional public loans from institutions such as the World Bank are generally much smaller than aid.

For India and Pakistan, the picture is somewhat different but not dissimilar. Private capital flows—both foreign direct investment and portfolio or equity investment—are greater than in the poorest countries on other continents. (In 1993, they totaled roughly $2 billion for India and half a billion for Pakistan—in contrast to respective aid flows of $1.5 billion and $1.1 billion.) But they are still modest. Nonconcessional loans from the World Bank and other institutions are available as well—about

$10 billion were disbursed to those two countries in 1993, for example. Adding all these sources of funds together, however, gross resource availability was only about $15 per person.

Given unstable political contexts, high levels of poverty, and fragile social situations, private capital flows in particular are unlikely to increase quickly to some of the regions mentioned above.[7] Countries can generate their own resources through savings and trade; indeed, even in poorer countries most investment does come from domestic savings. But properly timed international assistance can provide a significant impetus to the development process, as the east Asian examples demonstrate. We believe such an impetus is necessary, given the large percentage of the world's population that remains poor.

Moreover, demographic and environmental pressures are too great and international linkages in areas such as migration and terrorism too potentially dangerous to western interests for the international community to allow itself the luxury of demanding complete self-reliance from poorer states. The prospects of near-term success in controlling population growth, improving basic health and nutritional conditions, establishing sustainable economic growth, and avoiding or ending conflict in a number of regions hinge in large part on external support. It is out of concern for these countries and U.S. interests in them that this study is undertaken.

2

Development Aid
in Perspective

*D*EVELOPMENT ASSISTANCE, though only half a penny on the federal dollar, tries to do nearly as many types of things for countries overseas as the U.S. government does for its citizens here at home. In fact, it is in some ways even more complicated than that. There are dozens of important donors as well as more than 100 recipients together with their relevant official and nongovernmental agencies. To make sense of this complex web, it is useful to consider various slices of the global aid effort one at a time. But first we present the overall U.S. international affairs budget, including other types of foreign aid besides development assistance (figure 2-1 shows its magnitude within the overall U.S. federal budget).

The U.S. International Affairs Budget

Most federal funding for international activities is part of the so-called 150 federal budget account. Smaller pieces are in the defense budget and the agriculture budget, but they do not count as international spending and are not part of the dollar totals cited for international activities in this study.

The 150 account includes repayments to the U.S. government and other effects that can be thought of as negative spending (they reduce the deficit). For that reason, the 150 account is smaller in dollar terms than the so-called international discretionary budget. That latter accounting scheme, used in all budget legislation of the past decade and in Congress's 1996 budget-balancing plan, focuses on new responsibilities the government assumes.

Table 2-1 shows five main financial and functional categories of international spending. The categories are international development and

FIGURE 2-1. *U.S. Federal Spending by Category, 1996 and 2002: Projections Based on the President's Budget*

Percent of total spending[a]

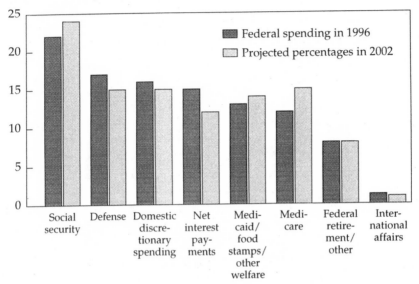

Sources: Congressional Budget Office, *Economic and Budget Outlook: Fiscal Years 1997–2006* (May 1996); Executive Office of the President, *Budget of the United States Government, Fiscal Year 1998: Historical Tables* (February 1997), p. 109.

a. These percentages add up to roughly 104; offsetting receipts (negative spending) bring the actual total back down to 100 percent. "Federal retirement" includes military pensions; "other" includes unemployment compensation. The "Medicaid/food stamps/other welfare" category includes the earned income tax credit. Each percent of current federal spending represents about $15 billion. The "projected percentages" show spending estimates for 2002 under the president's long-term budget.

humanitarian assistance, with 1997 outlays of about $8 billion; international security assistance, at $5.9 billion; conduct of foreign affairs ($4.1 billion); foreign information and exchange activities (just over $1 billion); and international financial programs ($0.4 billion). This study focuses on the first two categories, but also addresses the third and fourth to some extent. Official development aid includes almost all of the first category and about 40 percent of the second.

International development and humanitarian assistance includes funds for the U.S. Agency for International Development, the P.L. 480 food aid

TABLE 2-1. *President's Request for International Spending, Fiscal Years 1997, 1998*

U.S. $ billions

	FY 1997 estimate	FY 1998 request
Function 151		
International development and humanitarian aid	8.0	7.5
Multinational development banks; international		
organizations and programs	2.0	2.0
Development aid	2.3	2.1
Newly independent and central/eastern European		
states	1.2	1.2
P.L. 480 food aid	1.1	0.9
Refugee assistance	0.9	0.7
Peace Corps, other	0.5	0.6
Function 152		
International security assistance	5.9	6.1
Economic support fund	2.4	2.4
Foreign military financing (FMF)	3.3	3.5
Other	0.2	0.2
Function 153		
Conduct of foreign affairs	4.1	4.2
Function 154		
Foreign information and exchange activities	1.2	1.1
Function 155		
International financial programs	0.4	0.5
Total discretionary spending	19.6	19.3

Source: Executive Office of the President, *Budget of the United States Government, Fiscal Year 1998* (February 1997), pp. 252–253.

program for disaster relief and sale of U.S. agricultural surpluses, funds for multilateral development institutions such as the World Bank, the Peace Corps, refugee and humanitarian assistance, support for specialized UN agencies such as UNICEF, and assistance to the countries of central and eastern Europe. This latter element is not part of development aid as officially defined or as we define it in this study, but the other components are part of official development assistance (ODA).

International security assistance includes foreign military financing for purchases of U.S. arms and economic support funds; both go princi-pally to Israel and Egypt. The third category, conduct of foreign affairs, funds the State Department as well as U.S. dues for the UN's regular account and peacekeeping operations account. The fourth category, for-eign information and exchange activities, funds the U.S. Information Agency and National Endowment for Democracy and accounts for about 5 percent of the total. The last category, international financial programs, finances the Export-Import Bank and the U.S. contribution to the Inter-national Monetary Fund (the latter does not require actual expenditures, but does require budget authority).[1]

Outside of the 150 and international discretionary accounts, the United States also spends several hundred million dollars a year on the Nunn-Lugar program. That program, in effect since 1992 and also known as the cooperative threat reduction program with Russia and other former Soviet republics, is funded out of the Pentagon budget. A smaller, re-lated program is found in the Department of Energy. Both are within the so-called 050 account, and thus are part of national defense discretion-ary spending. Finally, the Pentagon and the 050 account pay for what are effectively additional and voluntary U.S. dues for UN peacekeep-ing—the costs of supporting UN peace operations or UN-authorized independent operations with the U.S. military (above and beyond the modest reimbursements that the United Nations provides the Pentagon for carrying out such services). Total costs were averaging roughly $1.5 billion a year of late (see table 2-2) but totaled about $3.5 billion in 1996 as a result of the peace implementation mission in Bosnia.[2]

U.S. Official Development Assistance

Figure 1-3 illustrates the history of U.S. development aid, the focus of this study, since 1960. This period may be thought of as roughly the era of the 1961 foreign assistance act.

Figure 1-3 displays what the Organization for Economic Cooperation and Development calls official development assistance (ODA). ODA includes all official grants and loans with development as their primary objective that are at least 25 percent concessional (by comparison with a market-based loan). Because most U.S. aid is grant aid, and most loans are highly concessional, U.S. ODA is essentially equal to federal outlays for development.

Overall federal outlays for international affairs have also declined, by

TABLE 2-2. *Costs of Unexpected Military Operations, Fiscal Years 1994, 1995*

U.S. $ millions

Countries	Fiscal year 1994 contingency operations' costs	Fiscal year 1995 contingency operations' costs
Bosnia	279	311.9
Cuba	107	370.1
Haiti	396	591.6
Korea	70	59
Rwanda	127	17.2
Somalia	520	17.3
Equipment replenishment and related		148.1
Southwest Asia		
Provide Comfort	92	122.5
Southern Watch	332	456.4
Vigilant Warrior		461.6
Total	1,923	2,556

Source: William J. Perry, secretary of defense, *Annual Report to the President and the Congress*, February 1995, pp. 39, 40.

roughly 15 percent since the 1980s (see figure 1-1). It is sometimes argued that the international affairs budget declined by half over that period. Although technically true, this statement is misleading. It takes as a starting point a year of unusually high budgets. It also focuses on budget authority, which varies more than outlays because of the periodic need to replenish borrowing authority of various international financial institutions and for other reasons. But it is true that international spending has declined very substantially in recent years and is likely to keep doing so.[3]

Also of note are Americans' charitable donations to nongovernmental development organizations, foundations, churches, universities, and the like. Some estimates of total donations are as high as $12 billion a year. If the calculation excludes activities that, however desirable on their own merits, might be characterized as cultural and religious exchanges rather than development efforts, the true figure is probably $2 billion to $3 bil-

A Half Penny on the Federal Dollar

TABLE 2-3. *Major Recipients of U.S. Official Development Assistance*[a]
Millions of constant 1997 dollars

Recipient	1970–71 average	Recipient	1980–81 average	Recipient	1993–94 average
India	1,580	Egypt	1,440	Israel	1,170
Vietnam	1,210	Israel	1,310	Egypt	770
Indonesia	900	India	380	El Salvador	450
Pakistan	570	Turkey	320	Somalia	380
Korea	520	Bangladesh	250	Haiti	280
Brazil	410	Indonesia	240	Philippines	200
Turkey	410	U.S. Pacific Islands	190	Columbia	150
Columbia	340	Pakistan	160	Jordan	140
Israel	190	El Salvador	110	India	140
Laos	180	Peru	100	Jamaica	130
U.S. Pacific Islands	170	Sudan	100	Ethiopia	120
Morocco	160	Somalia	100	Bolivia	120
Nigeria	150	Kenya	90	Bangladesh	100
Tunisia	150	Philippines	90	Rwanda	100
Thailand	130	Liberia	80	Peru	100

Source: Organization for Economic Co-operation and Development, *Development Assistance Report 1995* (Paris: OECD, 1996), p. A82.

a. Aid to Russia and other members of the former Soviet Union and Warsaw Pact is not considered official development assistance. Therefore, those countries do not appear in this table. Military aid and aid disbursed through multilateral organizations are not included in this table.

lion annually. Americans are by this measure (as a percent of GDP) slightly more generous than most other westerners. However, their total contributions as a percent of GDP are less than half that of the OECD average even when official and private flows are considered together.[4]

Geographic distributions of U.S. economic aid have shifted as well, largely as a result of the geopolitical and security concerns of the day. In the 1950s and 1960s, U.S. assistance focused largely on Asia, though in the 1960s it also was directed in substantial amounts to Latin America. By the mid-1970s, aid was focused more on the Middle East, though Central America, sub-Saharan Africa, and parts of Asia also received significant fractions of the total. The major recipients in the 1953–61 period were Korea, India, Vietnam, Pakistan, Turkey, Yugoslavia, and Taiwan. In the early 1990s, they included Israel, Egypt, El Salvador, and the Philippines (see table 2-3).[5] They now focus first and foremost on the Middle East, with Latin America and sub-Saharan Africa each

TABLE 2-4. *Major Recipients of All Types of U.S. Bilateral Aid, 1996*
Millions of dollars of obligations

Recipient	Amount	Recipient	Amount
Israel	3,000	Ethiopia	115
Egypt	2,270	Rwanda	110
Russia	320	Peru	95
Bosnia	310	Armenia	95
Ukraine	245	Bolivia	85
Jordan	180	West Bank/Gaza	75
India	160	Bangladesh	75
Haiti	125		
South Africa	125		

Source: U.S. Agency for International Development, *Congressional Presentation Summary Tables, Fiscal Year 1997* (July, 1996), pp. 38–41.

receiving considerable amounts of assistance as well, as shown in tables 2-4 and 2-5.

U.S. Development Strategies over Time

Different philosophies guided the way these dollars were provided from one period to another. In the 1950s and 1960s, donors, led by the United States, sought to transfer large amounts of resources principally for infrastructural investment. They provided specific technical help in areas such as agriculture, but their emphasis was largely on industry— even if the industry was not particularly efficiently managed, did not take advantage of a country's natural advantages, or was not functioning within a sensible macroeconomic framework. In countries such as

TABLE 2-5. *Distribution of U.S. Bilateral Aid, 1996*[a]
Percent of total obligations

Middle East and North Africa	Europe and former Soviet republics	Sub-Saharan Africa	Latin America and Caribbean	South Asia	Other Asia and Oceania
58	18	12	7	3	2

Source: U.S. Agency for International Development, *Congressional Presentation Summary Tables, Fiscal Year 1997* (July, 1996), pp. 37–39.

a. All U.S. bilateral aid including military assistance and assistance to newly independent states and central European countries is included (though it is not ODA).

South Korea and Taiwan that were prepared to make fundamental reforms while receiving those resources or that could be strongly influenced by U.S. suasion, this strategy worked. It also was successful in helping generate the so-called green revolution, in which agricultural research and extension produced new crop hybrids that more than doubled agricultural yield per acre in places like the Philippines, Mexico, and India.

But elsewhere, these strategies often produced a poor use of resources. Aid reformers in the 1970s grew frustrated with their inability to ease the continued plight of many of the world's poor. They decided to refocus resources and activities more directly on helping them through education, various employment schemes, and other projects. This thinking was juxtaposed with the growing recognition that explicit and broad-based help for the agricultural sector was a more important part of development than earlier believed.

By the 1980s, however, the limits of anti-poverty aid strategies were also recognized, as donors and many recipients saw that the well-being of most of the world's poor was inevitably dependent on broad-based economic growth. The contrast between countries that "got economic fundamentals right," especially the newly industrialized trade-oriented economies of east Asia, and many other developing states underscored the importance of sound macroeconomic policy for the poor as well as everyone else in a given society. The unusual economic characteristics of the 1970s, begun by oil shocks and concluded by the debt crisis, brought home these realities even more poignantly.

As a result, donors pressured recipients to institute austerity measures to reduce excessive consumer subsidies, correct misaligned exchange rates that benefited urban consumers to the detriment of agriculture and other potential export sectors, and trim excessively large government sectors that hindered economic performance. But the adjustments necessitated by macroeconomic distortions often had a short-term price for the poor. As the 1980s progressed, donors began to try to offset their negative effects with safety net measures to provide, for example, nutritional support and short-term employment opportunities.

Because of its declining fraction of total global aid donations and because of the growing capabilities of the international financial institutions, the United States also by this point was relying much more on the International Monetary Fund, World Bank, and related institutions to take the lead on structural adjustment efforts (see figure 2-2). Allowing

FIGURE 2-2. *U.S. Official Development Assistance through Multilateral Institutions, 1962–94*[a]

Billions of constant 1997 dollars

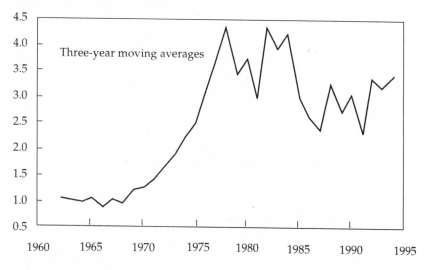

Source: Organization for Economic Co-operation and Development, *Development Co-operation, 1995* (Paris: OECD, 1996), p. A36, and other years.
a. U.S. contributions to multilateral institutions include grants and capital subscription payments to banks. The multilateral organizations administrating official development assistance (ODA) include: the World Bank Group, the International Development Bank, the Asian Development Bank, the African Development Fund, the Commission of the European Community, and United Nations agencies such as UNICEF and UNDP.

these institutions to handle difficult economic negotiations also provided useful political insulation to bilateral relationships. As the largest donor and the host country to their headquarters, the United States also retained great influence over these institutions and found it advantageous to rely more on multilateral approaches even for its own national purposes.[6]

The Macroeconomic Context

To be understood properly, the evolution of U.S. aid flows needs to be put in broader macroeconomic context. In the early postwar years there were few alternatives to aid for getting capital into developing countries. Private capital flows from the United States to developing coun-

FIGURE 2-3. *Net Flow of Private Capital to Developing Countries, 1960–94*[a]

Millions of constant 1997 dollars

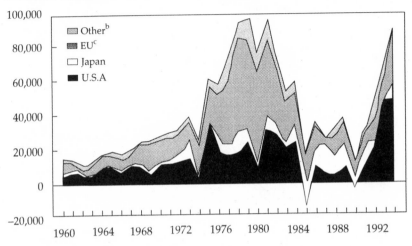

Sources: Organization for Economic Co-operation and Development, *Development Assistance Report 1995* (Paris: OECD, 1996), pp. A9–A10, and DAC reports from previous years for earlier data.

a. Private capital flows consist of flows financed out of private sector resources. They include direct investment, portfolio investment, bank loans, bank lending, and private export credits. The values for 1985 as well as 1990 reflect a net outflow of capital from developing countries to the United States.

b. "Other" includes Australia (missing data 1960–63), Canada, New Zealand (after 1970), Norway (missing data for 1960 and 1962), and Switzerland.

c. "EU" includes: Austria, Belgium, Denmark, Finland (after 1970), France, Germany, Ireland (after 1980), Italy, Netherlands, Luxembourg (after 1988), Portugal (for years 1964–70 and 1988–94), Spain (after 1988), Sweden, and the United Kingdom.

tries were small, totaling only about $5 billion annually in the early 1960s. By the mid-1970s, they often exceeded $20 billion a year. In the mid 1980s, however, the debt crisis reduced flows dramatically for a number of years. Recently, they have reached (and surpassed) the levels of the 1970s, as shown in figure 2-3. By 1995, total private flows to developing countries reached a historic high of $170 billion, nearly three times total global aid flows. But most of the private capital resources go to about twenty larger and wealthier developing countries.[7]

Trade, too, has grown significantly. Today half of all U.S. exports, valued at about $250 billion a year, go to countries outside the OECD. Altogether, developing countries are involved in trading about a trillion dollars of goods a year now—roughly a quarter of the world's total, and a factor of nearly ten greater than the level of four decades ago as measured in real dollars.[8] Again, however, trade helps some countries much more than others.

Other Types of U.S. Aid

In addition to official development assistance provided to the world's poorer countries, the United States also provides four other main types of assistance: economic and demilitarization aid to the states of central Europe and the former Soviet Union; information and exchange services to poorer and less free countries through international radio broadcasting as well as various exchange programs and democracy-building initiatives; military aid, principally to Israel and Egypt; and a large share of the international support for peace operations, both in direct dues to the United Nations and (even more so) in military backup for such operations.

In the early 1990s, aid to the former Soviet republics and central European states reached more than $2 billion a year. Since 1995 it has totaled about $1 billion a year (see table 2-6).[9] In 1994, the U.S. total was $2.4 billion; Germany provided $2.6 billion, France $650 million, the United Kingdom $300 million, and Japan and Austria each about $250 million.[10] This money is different from aid to the least-developed countries, which have much lower per capita income levels and often few near-term prospects of attracting substantial amounts of foreign capital. In Russia and other similar countries, aid is intended to facilitate the shift to market-oriented economies and to ameliorate the social costs of those transitions in the short term—until improvements from foreign and domestic private capital result.

For decades, the United States has tried to promote democracy, strengthen civil and political institutions overseas, and in some cases undermine the power of autocratic regimes through various information and exchange programs. Although it has been reduced substantially in recent years, funding for these programs remains at about $1.2 billion a year. Like assistance to the central and east European states, it is within the international discretionary budget.

Military aid, now part of the international discretionary budget, peaked at more than $30 billion a year in the early 1950s. After a sustained decline, it approached $20 billion a year during the "Vietnamization" ef-

TABLE 2-6. *U.S. Bilateral Assistance to Former Soviet Republics, 1991–96*[a]
Millions of dollars

	Cumulative budget authority (through FY 1996)	Cumulative obligations (as of 3/31/96)	Cumulative outlays (as of 3/31/96)
USAID	3,350	2,700	1,915
Department of Commerce	35	25	20
Overseas Private Investment Corp.	95	70	—
USIA Freedom Support Act exchanges	270	190	190
U.S. Trade & Development Agency	50	40	25
U.S. Department of Energy	180	130	55
Humanitarian shipments (U.S. government and private)	130	130	130
Other agencies[b]	245	180	140
Export-Import Bank	400	300	—
Cooperative threat reduction funds	1,525	990	480
Other DOD funds	30	0	0
U.S. Department of Agriculture	2,730	2,730	2,730
Total	9,040	7,485	5,580
Total in 1997 dollars	9,700	8,000	5,800

Source: Official of Richard L. Morningstar, Coordinator of U.S. Assistance to the NIS, "U.S. Government Assistance to and Cooperative Activities with the New Independent States of the Former Soviet Union, October 1995–March 1996," (1996), Appendix.

a. The estimated value of nonfood aid cargo, which includes private donations plus excess Defense Department articles, is not included in these data but totals more than one billion dollars. Figures are rounded to the nearest five million dollars.

b. Includes the U.S. Nuclear Regulatory Commission, Peace Corps, U.S. Department of Treasury, and other bureaus.

fort of the early 1970s, but then declined to a level typically around $5 billion.[11] It has diminished further in recent years in the wake of the cold war, becoming essentially a tool of supporting the Mideast peace process and to a much lesser extent of facilitating NATO's Partnership for Peace program. About 90 percent of its $3.3 billion annual total is provided to Israel and Egypt.

Military aid has been provided through a variety of programs and organizations, including the former Military Assistance Program, International Military Education and Training, transfer of excess defense goods, and Foreign Military Financing (the latter now the dominant element in dollar terms). It does not include the Economic Support Fund, which is considered part of official development assistance and provides the other $2 billion in annual U.S. aid to Israel and Egypt.

As used here, "military aid" also does not include the funds for security-related objectives provided out of the military budget. These programs include the Nunn-Lugar cooperative threat reduction program and the Department of Energy's lab-to-lab partnerships and other efforts. Funds for these purposes have totaled about half a billion dollars a year in the 1990s.

Finally, the United States continues to provide funds for UN peace operations as well as direct bilateral military support for those operations. Its dues have averaged about half a billion dollars a year in this decade, and its costs for U.S. military activities supporting various UN peace operations about $2 billion.

Totaling these four categories of non-ODA assistance, the United States now provides another $6 billion a year in various types of aid within the international discretionary budget. It also provides about $2 billion to $4 billion a year in assistance to other countries through the defense budget. Specifically, it provides Nunn-Lugar cooperative threat reduction assistance to the former Soviet republics and military backup for various multilateral peace operations. All of this aid combined thus nearly equals the nation's ODA at present.

U.S. Assistance in International Perspective

The United States was once the dominant provider of official development assistance to poorer countries, but by the early 1990s it provided only about one-sixth of the global total (see figure 2-4). In fact, by 1995 the U.S. contribution had slipped to about one-eighth of the world total, or $7.3 billion out of $59 billion (in then-year or nominal dollars).[12]

The United States makes out less well if one considers its aid as a percentage of gross domestic product (GDP). By this index, it has been the least generous official provider of aid within the OECD. In 1995 the United States devoted only about 0.10 percent of its GDP to official development assistance, while all OECD providers as a whole averaged 0.27 percent, as shown in figure 2-5. (This means that, excluding the United States, other donors provided on average 0.35 percent of GDP— or half of the official UN goal, and roughly the level that has characterized total global aid since the 1970s.)[13]

FIGURE 2-4. *Official Development Assistance[a] by All Donors, 1959–95*

Billions of constant 1997 dollars

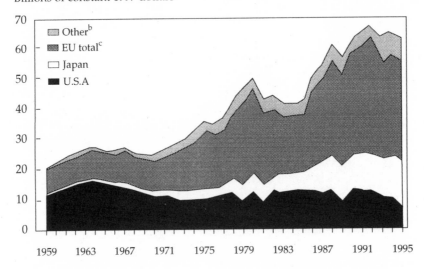

Source: Organization for Economic Co-operation and Development, *Development Co-operation: Aid in Transition 1995* (Paris: OECD, 1996), and other years.

a. Official Development Assistance (ODA) refers to grants or loans undertaken by the official sector with promotion of economic development and welfare as the main objectives, and at concessional financial terms (a loan must have a grant element of at least 25 percent). The decrease in U.S. ODA in 1995 was partially due to delays in approving the U.S. budget for FY 1996, which held up an estimated $1 billion in payments to Israel and $0.7 billion in capital subscriptions to multilateral development banks.

b. "Other" includes: Australia (after 1960), Canada, New Zealand (after 1970), Norway, Switzerland (after 1960), and Saudi Arabia, Kuwait and UAE (after 1985).

c. EU includes: Austria (after 1960), Belgium, Denmark, Finland (after 1970), France, Germany, Ireland (after 1980), Italy, Netherlands, Luxembourg (after 1988), Portugal (for years 1960–70 and 1988–94), Spain (after 1988), Sweden (after 1960), and the United Kingdom.

Japan provides by far the most aid of any country, an amount that exceeded $14 billion or roughly one-fourth of the global total in 1995 (see table 2-7). Even allowing for the fact that much of its aid is given in the form of concessional loans, the grant-equivalent value of its aid was roughly $12 billion, by far the greatest total by this measure as well. France and Germany each provided slightly more money than the United States—though slightly less if adjustment is made for delayed payments resulting from the U.S. budget crisis.

FIGURE 2-5. *Economic Burden of Foreign Aid by Donor, 1995*[a]

Percentage of gross national product

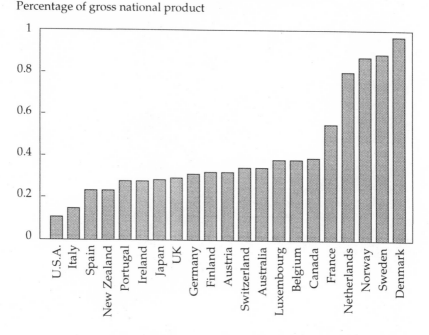

Source: Organization for Economic Co-operation and Development, "Financial Flows to Developing Countries in 1995: Sharp Decline in Official Aid; Private Flows Rise," Press Release (OECD, 1996) p. 12.

a. These figures represent the actual grant component (as opposed to the nominal face-value) of loans and other forms of official development assistance.

A number of other European Community members and other countries such as Norway, Switzerland, Canada, and Saudi Arabia are also important donors. Many of the European countries including France, Germany, the Scandinavian states, and the low countries are substantially more generous than the United States or Japan by the aid/GDP index, as shown in figure 2-5 and table 2-7.[14] Thinking in terms of geographic blocs, Europe provides half of all aid, Japan and the United States most of the rest.

Some countries, such as France, emphasize bilateral programs; others, like Germany, work largely through multilateral channels such as the banks and the United Nations Development Program (see figure 2-6). France and Britain focus to an extent on former colonies. Europe as a

TABLE 2-7. *Foreign Aid Donations by OECD Countries, 1995*[a]
Constant 1997 $ billion, unless otherwise specified

Donor country	Net official ODA, 1995 (current $ billion)	Net official ODA	ODA as percent of GNP	Estimated grant-equivalent value of ODA
Japan	14.5	15.1	.28	12.0
France	8.4	8.8	.55	7.5
Germany	7.5	7.8	.31	7.0
United States	7.3	7.6	.10	7.5
Netherlands	3.3	3.4	.80	3.0
United Kingdom	3.2	3.3	.29	3.0
Canada	2.1	2.2	.39	2.0
Sweden	2.0	2.1	.89	2.0
Denmark	1.6	1.7	.97	—
Italy	1.5	1.6	.14	1.5
Spain	1.3	1.4	.23	1.0
Norway	1.24	1.3	.87	1.0
Australia	1.14	1.2	.34	1.0
Switzerland	1.08	1.13	.34	1.0
Belgium	1.03	1.07	.38	1.0
Austria	.75	0.8	.32	0.5
Finland	.39	0.4	.32	0.5
Portugal	.27	.28	.27	—
Ireland	.14	.15	.27	.15
New Zealand	.12	.13	.23	.10
Luxembourg	.07	.07	.38	.05

Sources: Organization for Economic Co-operation and Development, *Development Co-operation, 1995* (Paris: OECD, 1996), pp. A4 and A47; and Organization for Economic Co-operation and Development, "Financial Flows to Developing Countries in 1995: Sharp Decline in Official Aid; Private Flows Rise," Press Release, (OECD, 1996).

a. Since some aid is given as loans at concessional rates, its grant-equivalent component is less than the nominal size of the loan. Thus, a country's actual aid is generally somewhat smaller than its ODA. Here, the estimates of grant aid are approximate. They apply the grant-like aid ratios of 1993–94 to 1995 ODA.

TABLE 2-8. *Regional Distribution of Official Development Assistance by Donor, 1993–94*

Percent of total gross disbursements

Country/ donor group	Sub-Saharan Africa	South and Central Asia	Other Asia and Oceania	Middle East, North Africa, and southern Europe	Latin America and Caribbean
U.S.	21	8	4	42	25
Japan	14	23	31	20	12
EU	45	9	9	24	13
IFIs[a]	45	35	8	3	9
UN agencies	44	13	6	25	14
Total	37	15	11	23	14

Source: Organization for Economic Co-operation and Development, *Development Assistance Report 1995* (Paris: OECD, 1996), pp. A59–A60.

a. International financial institutions.

whole focuses on Africa more than does the United States—which gives a fair amount of money to the Middle East and Latin America—or Japan, which focuses largely on Southeast, South, and southwest Asia (see table 2-8). But they all wind up giving roughly comparable fractions of their total aid to the less-developed and least-developed countries.[15]

Japan provides substantially more of its aid in loans, and somewhat more for economic infrastructure, than the typical donor. More than most, it uses aid to gain an economic foothold in developing countries. But Japan still provides more than two-thirds of its aid for social programs, agriculture, and other more grass-roots–oriented efforts. The United States and Canada give more food aid than the average, but that aid still represents less than 10 percent of their total assistance efforts.

As noted, the United States gave $7.3 billion in so-called official development assistance in 1995. That number is misleadingly low, however; the budget crisis delayed a total of $1.7 billion in payments to Israel and to the multilateral development banks that normally would have been made at the end of calendar year 1995 but were postponed (though ultimately paid).

U.S. assistance looks more generous if one also considers the non-ODA aid discussed above. As noted, about $6 billion is provided out of the

FIGURE 2-6. *Bilateral and Multilateral Aid from the Development Assistance Committee Members, 1994*[a]

Percent; billions of U.S. dollars in parentheses

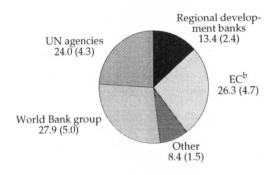

Multilateral (17.9)

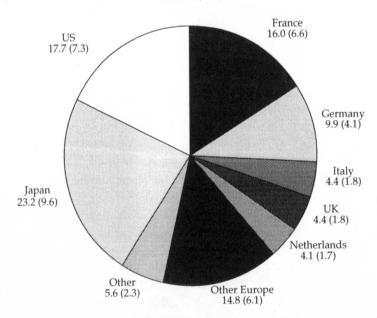

Bilateral (41.3)

Source: Organization for Economic Co-operation and Development, *Development Assistance Report 1995* (Paris: OECD, 1996), pp. A21–A22, A39–A40.

a. The largest contributors to multilateral aid efforts were Japan (21 percent of the total), Germany (15 percent), the United States (15 percent), France (10 percent), the United Kingdom (8 percent), and Italy (5 percent).

b. EC refers to the commission of the European Community.

international discretionary category, including dues for peacekeeping and U.S. Information Agency activities and military aid; another $2 billion or so comes from the Pentagon budget. Other donors typically give less, even as a percent of their GDP, within these categories. Together, they roughly double the size of the U.S. assistance budget broadly defined, resulting in total contributions of about 0.2 percent of GDP. Other donors, who on average give 0.35 percent of GDP as ODA, give no more than 0.40 percent when these other categories are included. Japan's contributions in particular do not rise much by this accounting scheme, totaling perhaps 0.30 percent of GDP rather than 0.28 percent in ODA terms. Viewed thus broadly, the United States is essentially tied for first with Japan in its absolute level of assistance to foreign countries—though it still gives much less than average as a percent of GDP.[16]

There are additional reasons to temper the frequently heard argument that the United States is somehow shirking a moral obligation by providing less development aid as a percent of its GDP than do other western states. First of all, it provided more than half of all aid in earlier decades, beginning with the Marshall Plan and continuing into the 1960s—suggesting that it is perhaps not unreasonable that it provide a bit less than its share now. In addition, U.S. military spending—good not only for other western states, but for the developing countries that rely on a stable and peaceful international environment to conduct trade and otherwise benefit from the global economic system that is their best route to economic growth—is considerably more as a percent of GDP than that of its allies (see table 2-9.) Finally, it also has relatively open markets. Thus the burden-sharing argument as commonly heard appears rather weak—or, at a minimum, overused.

Other types of arguments to the same end are more convincing, however. For example, if global aid flows today are insufficient, as we argue below that they are, the United States is hardly likely to catalyze an increase in them without being willing to provide more resources itself—or at a minimum to stabilize its aid budget, now in rapid decline. If it fails to do so, it can also expect to have increasing difficulty in galvanizing international efforts for activities such as the reconstruction of Bosnia or development of the West Bank and the Gaza Strip. In addition, should the United States wish to retain the extensive influence it still holds in development circles, particularly in the international financial institutions, it would be wise not to let its aid drop further as a percent of the global total.

TABLE 2-9. *Overall Foreign Policy Spending as Percent of GDP, 1995*

	NATO Europe (excluding Greece and Turkey)	Canada, Australia, New Zealand, Sweden, Switzerland, and Austria	Japan	United States
Official development assistance[a]	0.37	0.34	0.28	0.10
Other aid-related activities including peacekeeping (approximate)	0.075	0.025	0.01	0.1
Defense spending	2.3	2.0	1.0	3.9
Total	2.7	2.4	1.3	4.1

Sources: Organization for Economic Co-operation and Development, "Financial Flows to Developing Countries in 1995," June 11, 1996; Stockholm International Peace Research Institute, *SIPRI Yearbook 1996* (Oxford, England: Oxford University Press, 1996), pp. 365–70; International Institute for Strategic Studies, *The Military Balance 1995–1996* (New York: Oxford University Press, 1995), p. 39; World Bank, *World Development Report 1995* (New York: Oxford University Press, 1995), p.196.

a. The U.S. figure for official development assistance would be 0.12 percent of GDP if adjusted for aid disbursed later than usual because of the U.S. budget crisis.

Recipients of Development Assistance

The $59 billion official global aid budget in 1995 (nearly $62 billion when expressed in 1997 dollars) was intended in one way or another to serve much of the world's roughly 4.5 billion people who live outside the countries of the Organization for Economic Cooperation and Development and a few other places. On average, that works out to about $15 per person per year. But which countries actually got the most money, in absolute terms and, more important, on a per capita basis?

In one way the distribution of official development assistance looks very sensible, as indicated in figure 2-7. Of the aid easily broken down in these terms, nearly three-fourths went to "less-developed countries" with the lowest incomes; most of the remainder to the so-called lower–middle-income countries (such as Bolivia, El Salvador, Senegal, Thailand, and Turkey), which are generally still quite poor; and only a very small amount to the wealthier developing countries (such as Brazil, Botswana, Malaysia, Mexico, and Venezuela).

FIGURE 2-7. *Receipts of Foreign Aid from All Donors, by Income Group, 1993*[a]

Billions of U.S. dollars

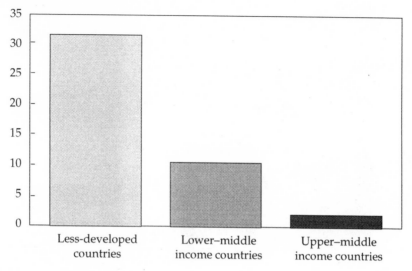

Source: World Bank, *World Development Report 1995* (N.Y.: Oxford University Press, 1995), pp. 198–99.

a. Less-developed countries had a per capita GNP less than $700 in 1993; lower–middle income countries had a per capita GNP between $700 and $3,000; and upper–middle income countries had a per capita GNP between $3,000 and $10,000.

Some aid was not clearly attributed to a specific recipient and therefore is not included in this chart. The aid total for lower–middle income countries does not include figures for the former Soviet republics or several East European states, even though they technically belong in that category. Aid to Israel, a high-income economy, which totaled $1.3 billion in 1993, is not included here. Aid refers to official development assistance.

As figure 2-8 and figure 2-9 show, Africa, the poorer regions of the Middle East, and the Caribbean and Central American states receive disproportionately more aid than do other regions of the developing world, particularly on a per capita basis. Asia, with the general exception of the Pacific island states, gets notably less.

Although one might consider this distribution sensible, African countries and many of the world's island states in the Pacific and the Caribbean get a great deal of aid partly because there are so many of them. Simply put, donors disburse aid less by recipient individual than by re-

FIGURE 2-8. *Regional Distribution of Official Development Assistance from All Donors, 1993/1994*

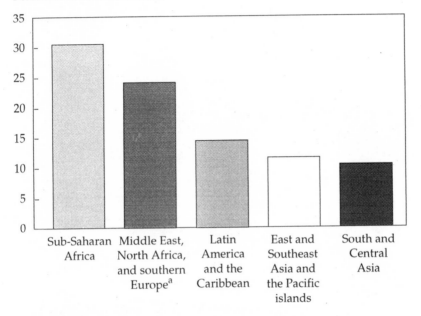

Percent of total disbursements

Source: Organization for Economic Co-operation and Development, *Development Assistance Report, 1995* (Paris: OECD, 1996), pp. A59–A60.

a. Aid recipients in southern Europe are Turkey, Cyprus, states of the former Yugoslavia, Malta, Albania, and Gibraltar.

cipient country. Perhaps they feel that assistance can buy political influence in small countries; perhaps their aid missions care more about the percent of the world's countries they set foot in than about the effectiveness of their programs in larger nations. Whatever the explanation, larger poor states generally do not make out well on the aid front.

For example, India, Pakistan, and Bangladesh together have well over 1 billion people—about one-fourth of the developing world's population, and including more than one-third of its poorest. But they received only about $4 billion in 1993, less than 10 percent of total global foreign aid and a very small amount in per capita terms (see table 2-10).[17] China is similar to the above group in its population, and it gets even less of the global aid budget (and no U.S. aid, except a tiny amount in the form of a

FIGURE 2-9. *Foreign Aid per Capita, from All Donors, by Region, 1994*[a]

Receipts in billions of U.S. dollars

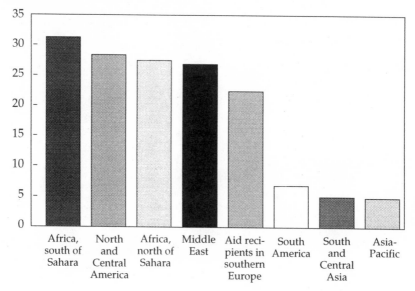

Source: Organization for Economic Co-operation and Development, *Development Assistance Report, 1995* (Paris: OECD, 1996), pp. A53–A56.

a. "Foreign Aid" refers to grants or loans undertaken by the official sector with promotion of economic development and welfare as the main objectives and at concessional financial terms (the loans must have a grant element of at least 25 percent). China and the Pacific islands, as well as Southeast Asian countries, are included in the Asia-Pacific category; Egypt and Algeria are included in Africa, north of Sahara; the Caribbean is included in North and Central America; and Myanmar is considered part of south and Central Asia. Aid recipients in southern Europe are Albania, Cyprus, Gibraltar, Malta, Turkey, and the states of the former Yugoslavia.

small Peace Corps presence). It has other extensive sources of hard currency—exports, commercial loans, and private investment funds— whereas most states on the Indian subcontinent do not (see figure 2-10, which also reveals the small flows of private capital to Africa as well as the Mideast region.)

Thus, though the less-developed countries get at least two-thirds of all aid as a group, the subgroup of small states with an aggregate population of about 1 billion gets most of that amount; they received $24 billion of the roughly $31 billion given to the poorest countries in 1993.

TABLE 2-10. *Foreign Aid per Capita from All Sources, for Selected Recipients,*
1993[a]

Recipient	Per capita aid	Percent of per capita GNP
India	$1.70	0.6
Nigeria	$2.70	0.9
China	$2.80	0.8
Pakistan	$8.70	2.1
Bangladesh	$12.00	5.8
Average for all other less-developed countries[b]	$35.35	10.0
Average for lower–middle income countries[c]	$16.60	1.2
Average for upper–middle income countries[d]	$10.20	0.2

Source: World Bank, *World Development Report 1995* (New York: Oxford University Press, 1995), pp. 162–63 and 198–99.

a. "Aid" refers to official development assistance. Total official development assistance per capita amounted to $40.80 for Egypt and $242.50 for Israel (not including U.S. military aid to either country).

b. All less-developed countries not listed individually have populations below 100 million.

c. LMICs have per capita incomes between $700 and $3,000 per year.

d. UMICs have per capita incomes between $3,000 and $10,000 per year.

China, India, Bangladesh, Pakistan, and Nigeria, with about 2.5 billion people among them, received only $7 billion.[18]

Private capital, always important for developing countries, has become dramatically more important of late. In 1990, net private capital flows to developing countries, including the states of central and eastern Europe and central Asia, totaled $44 billion, comparable to the prevailing level of foreign aid. In 1995, despite a slowing in the rate of growth that affected most parts of the developing world after the Mexican peso crisis in 1994, the level was $167 billion, or more than two and a half times all official development assistance. Declines in portfolio (stock) investment that occurred in 1994 and 1995 were more than offset by increases in foreign direct investment and commercial bank lending. The largest increase during the 1990–95 period was in China, where net private capital flows increased from $8 billion to $45 billion. Substantial increases, many of them greater on a per capita basis, also were witnessed in South Korea ($1.1 billion in 1990, $16.5 billion in 1995), Malaysia ($1.6 billion to $12.1 billion), Argentina (-$0.2 billion to $8.8 billion),

FIGURE 2-10. *Recent Capital Flows to Developing Countries, from All Sources*[a]
Billions of U.S. dollars

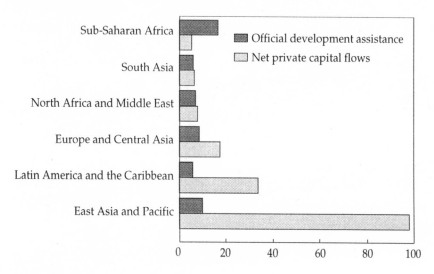

Sources: Organization for Economic Co-operation and Development, *Development Co-operation 1995* (Paris: OECD, 1996), pp. A67, A96; World Bank, *World Debt Tables*, vol. 1 (Washington, D.C.: World Bank 1996), p. 11.

a. Aid figures are annual averages for the two-year period 1993–94, the most recent for which data are available; private flows are for 1995.

Indonesia ($3.3 billion to $11.4 billion), Brazil ($0.5 billion to $6.9 billion), Thailand ($4.7 billion to $8.2 billion), and elsewhere. In contrast, annual flows grew by only $15 billion over that period for sub-Saharan Africa, the Middle East and North Africa, and south Asia combined.[19]

Exports also provide hard currency, though for most low-income countries they are insufficient to cover the cost of imports (many of which correspond to basic capital goods needed for economic development or basic health and nutritional needs). For example, among the forty-five lowest-income countries excluding China, India, Nigeria, Pakistan, and Bangladesh, exports totaled less than $25 billion in 1993—nearly equal to their total aid and well below their $40 billion in imports that year.[20]

The large amount of economic development aid resources flowing to Africa, generally totaling several hundred million dollars a year per country from all sources, calls into question an assertion frequently made by aid proponents: that by spending more on aid now, we will tend to spend less on conflict resolution later. To be sure, it is better on humanitarian grounds to prevent conflict. And, in a specific country's case, it is true that a massive military or humanitarian intervention would generally cost up to several times more than aid during the period of intense operations. And someday it may be true that overpopulation or environmental degradation in Africa will cause more calamitous global effects— though the odds of such an occurrence cannot be analytically established.

At present, however, Africa receives some $20 billion a year in aid and costs outside powers no more than a few billion dollars a year in military operations. UN peacekeeping costs are generally less than $1 billion annually; even in the years of the Somalia operations, they were about $2 billion. The additional costs of unilateral operations by the large powers are on that order as well. Even if one factors in all the costs of refugee assistance and humanitarian relief, the so-called complex humanitarian disasters cost less than $10 billion a year in Africa, while development aid (after subtracting emergency relief) totals about $15 billion. Although there are plenty of good reasons to stop violence through preventive action, achieving near-term cost savings is generally not one of them.

Uses And Effects of Development Assistance

Among the many uses to which foreign aid dollars are put—building bridges and roads and ports, paying civil servants and teachers, supplying health clinics, helping countries meet balance-of-payments requirements, relieving acute humanitarian crisis through provision of food, water, shelter, and the like—where do the dollars really go, and in what amounts?

In broad brush, aid may be seen as divided roughly one-third for basic human needs addressed through grass-roots efforts. These include disaster relief, child immunizations, local nutrition programs, and primary health care for mothers and babies. The other two-thirds funds countrywide programs and macroeconomic development in such forms as help for education, infrastructure construction projects, targeted environmental initiatives, and balance of payments assistance (whether in the form of cash or of food aid that can be sold locally to generate revenue). The subcategories that make up these totals can be seen, at least roughly, by the imperfect but still helpful organizing scheme used by

FIGURE 2-11. *Major Uses of Foreign Aid, 1975–76, 1992–93*[a]

Percent of total

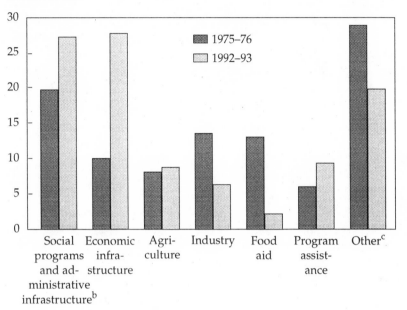

Source: Organization for Economic Co-operation and Development, *Development Assistance Report 1995* (OECD, 1996), p. A43.

a. This graph represents foreign aid provided by Development Assistance Committee (DAC) members and multilateral organizations. See table 2-7 for list of members. The figures shown include approximately $1 billion in debt forgiveness by the United States for military-related loans and approximately $1 billion in debt forgiveness by various countries for general export credits in 1992.

b. Includes education, health care, and water supply improvement.

c. Includes export credits.

the Organization for Economic Cooperation and Development and shown in figure 2-11.[21]

Fortunately, more detailed breakdowns are available for bilateral aid. They can be used to understand the broad categories shown in the figure for that 70 percent of all aid disbursed bilaterally in 1993. Roughly 25 percent of the bilateral aid was spent on social and administrative infrastructure, mostly to education, water resources, health care, and family planning. Another 20 percent went to major infrastructure, roughly evenly divided between energy on the one hand and transport

TABLE 2-11. *Trends in Human Development by Region, Selected Years, 1960–92*

	Sub-Saharan Africa	Arab states	South Asia[a]	East Asia[b]	South-east Asia	Latin America and the Caribbean
Life expectancy[c]						
1960	40.0	46.7	43.8	47.5	45.3	56.0
1992	51.1	64.3	58.5	70.5	62.9	67.7
Infant mortality[d]						
1960	165	165	164	146	126	105
1992	101	54	94	27	55	47
Access to safe water[e]						
1975–80	25	71	—	—	15	60
1988–91	45	79	—	—	53	79
Malnourished children[f]						
1975	31	25	69	26	46	17
1990	31	20	59	21	34	10
Adult literacy[e]						
1970	28	30	33	—	67	76
1992	51	57	47	—	86	86
Real GDP per capita[g]						
1960	—	1,310	700	730	1,000	2,140
1991	—	4,420	1,260	3,210	3,420	5,360

Source: United Nations Development Program, *Human Development Report 1994* (New York: Oxford University Press, 1994), p. 207

a. Includes Afghanistan, Bangladesh, Bhutan, India, Iran, Maldives, Nepal, Pakistan, and Sri Lanka.

b. China, Hong Kong, North Korea, South Korea, and Mongolia.

c. Years.

d. Per 1,000; deaths before first birthday.

e. Percent.

f. Percent; under age five.

g. In 1991 dollars; purchasing power parity (PPP) measure. The PPP gives a better indication of actual purchasing power for goods produced and consumed locally than does GDP calculated strictly according to the official exchange rate.

and communications on the other. About 12 percent went to various economic activities, principally agriculture (8 percent of aid total) and industry, mining, and construction (3 percent). About 10 percent of aid went to debt relief, 14 percent to program and institutional assistance or multisector projects, 3 percent to food aid, 6 percent to nonfood emergency aid, and the rest to donor costs or various and sundry unspecified efforts.[22]

FIGURE 2-12. *Fertility Rates Worldwide, Selected Years, 1962–92*

Fertility rate[a]

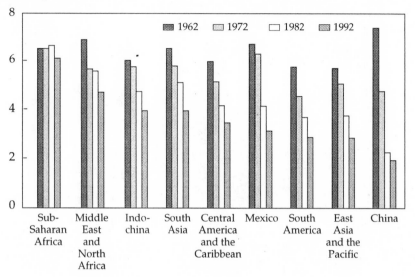

Sources: Congressional Budget Office, "Assessing Threats To U.S. Security," unpublished paper, May, 1995, based on CD-ROM data from the World Bank.

a. Total fertility rate shows the number of children that would be born alive to a woman during her lifetime if she were to live to the end of her childbearing years and bear children at each age in accordance with prevailing age-specific fertility rates. Estimates are made by the World Bank from data provided by the United Nations Population Division, the United Nations Statistical Office, and country statistical offices. The data are a combination of observed values and interpolated and projected estimates for each particular year. Data for each country are weighted by the country's share of the region's population.

The amount of all aid that goes for basic needs turns out to be about one-third of the total, or roughly $20 billion a year. It includes disaster relief, smaller-scale projects for water supply and sanitation, some health care, other social services, and a part of agricultural aid. Clearly not counted within this one-third are debt relief, program and institutional assistance, major infrastructure, most education, and much of the economic development category as well as various multisector or unspecified projects. A discussion of their overall effectiveness is reserved for chapters 3 and 4.

FIGURE 2-13. *Infant Mortality Rates for Selected Countries and Regions, 1962–92*[a]

Deaths per 1,000 live births

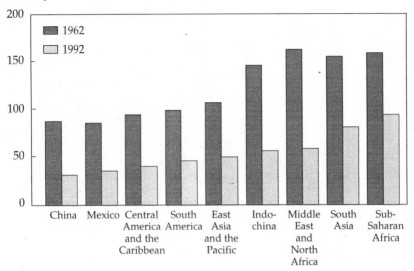

Sources: Congressional Budget Office, "Assessing Threats To U.S. Security," unpublished paper, May, 1995, based on CD-ROM data from the World Bank.

a. Infant mortality rates show the number of deaths of infants under one year of age per 1,000 live births in a given year. Data are a combination of observed values based on censuses or surveys and interpolated and extrapolated estimates for each particular year. Data for each country are weighted by the country's share of the region's population.

The basic grass-roots objectives to which aid has been put appear to have been partially accomplished. In conjunction with the efforts of recipient countries and other factors, aid has helped increase life expectancy in the developing world by well over ten years in every region since 1960, largely as a function of declining infant mortality rates. Population growth rates, though still very high in places, have also declined substantially; the typical woman of childbearing age in the developing world now has two fewer babies than was the case thirty years ago.

At least some of the credit for these positive developments is due to aid for increasing the availability of immunization services, oral rehydration mixes, contraceptives and family planning counseling, and greater literacy—particularly for women, who when educated for even a few years show marked declines in typical lifetime fertility rates. Foreign technical and financial assistance has helped in other ways as well (see table 2-11 and figures 2-12 and 2-13), such as by helping develop new plant hybrids through internationally supported agricultural research.

Recipient governments tend to spend about 5 percent of their GDP on health and education, for example, or on average roughly $20 per capita per year in the poorer countries. Donors provide about one-third of their total assistance funds for such purposes, as noted, or roughly $10 per recipient person in the major aid-receiving countries.[23] Often the efforts of recipients and donors are complementary; donors might satisfy the hard-currency requirements of a project, while recipients provide much of the necessary local labor.

3

Aid Effectiveness:
How to Define It?
How to Achieve It?

*H*ow well has development aid worked so far, and what does that tell us about how we should redesign it in the future? In this chapter, we argue that economic growth should be the principal goal of most development assistance, except those amounts provided to alleviate human suffering or directly support grass-roots programs. We summarize what is now known about aid's effectiveness in achieving the goal of macroeconomic growth.

Most Development Aid Should Focus on Promoting Growth

Growth is clearly not the sole objective of U.S. development aid. Indeed, it may be among the least important for many policymakers concerned with security, financial solvency, human rights, or democracy.[1] But while economic growth is not a sufficient condition for meeting all of the other objectives of aid, in most cases it is a necessary condition.[2] Moreover, asking aid to serve too many masters and trying to fine-tune its allocation as a function of multiple criteria risks muddying the waters so much that no purposes are well served.

For example, making slight adjustments in aid flows as a function of detailed political trends within a country makes little sense. It seems more appropriate to consider withdrawing aid in cases of blatant and worsening political or human rights abuses, but otherwise not to burden it with too many objectives.[3]

Even in extreme cases, donors may need to be flexible, providing recipients an opportunity to adjust policies before penalizing them. Pressure appears to have worked fairly well in this manner in the case of

President Fujimori in Peru, for example. After Peru imposed martial law, aid was suspended until elections were held for individuals charged with drafting a new constitution to guide the bodies Fujimori had disbanded. Thereafter, aid flows were reinstated.[4] Aid may also be provided to countries such as Indonesia, where, despite regrettable abuses at various points in its history, a strong state has arguably been important for maintaining internal order and advancing human development. External help also seems appropriate in places such as Rwanda, Ethiopia, Jordan, and Israel, where government abuses of human rights continue but appear to be diminishing.[5]

There is a good case on moral and pragmatic grounds for ending most aid to regimes that blatantly and unjustifiably abuse human rights or repudiate their citizens' political rights on a large scale. Examples might be Albania, Burma, the Sudan, and Zaire.[6] At a certain scale of atrocities, the promise of growth may become less attainable within a country regardless of its economic policies—and less important to a country's citizens than their basic physical security. But countries with such abysmal human rights policies tend to have bad economic policies as well, although there are exceptions. So one can still think of conditionality as primarily a tool of economic policy influence.

Aid for specialized economic purposes, such as support for microenterprises in developing countries, is important. But it should not become the main focus of future efforts. Absent a sound economic framework and functioning market in a recipient country, few such efforts can work. When sound economic fundamentals are in place, by contrast, there will be little reason for donors not to work with the recipient government. Moreover, the private sector simply cannot supplant recipient governments as the developer of certain public services such as health and education.

Likewise, aid for environmental protection should be restricted to narrowly tailored programs costing limited amounts of money. A good example is the effort to help developing countries eliminate use of ozone-depleting chemicals. But larger initiatives are unlikely to be effective unless recipients have sound economic and demographic policies. By the time developing countries are able to pollute on a scale of international consequence, they will usually be at a stage of development where tools besides official development assistance (ODA) can help them address their environmental concerns. Private capital, nonconcessional public capital, and their own resources should allow them to address most environmental challenges on their own. If they do not, trade levers may be the best way to induce compliance.

Finally, trying to use aid to create large markets for U.S. goods is bound to fail unless the principal aid objective of economic growth is achieved. There may be a modest benefit to ensuring that U.S. businessmen and contractors gain a foothold in a country as soon as those from other donor nations. This may be an argument for some type of robust bilateral development effort on those grounds, but that is about as far as the argument goes.

The "Conditionality" Paradigm

The objectives driving the allocation of aid have evolved considerably in the past half century. In the 1960s and 1970s, even development aid was driven primarily by cold war security concerns, with an underlying focus on poverty reduction. During the debt crisis of the 1980s, the rationale for aid shifted to limiting the liability that escalating developing country debts placed on the international economic system by enhancing the capacity of those countries to repay billions of dollars in debt. In the late 1980s and early 1990s, this rationale remained in place, along with an increasing emphasis on using aid to support the development of export markets and trading partners in the developing countries. Yet at the same time, as the human costs of the decade-long debt crisis became clear, the 1960s emphasis on poverty reduction resurfaced. It was made more complex by a new and accompanying emphasis on promoting democratic governance and human rights.[7]

Furthermore, the way in which donors have tried to use aid to promote the specific goal of economic development has varied from one period to another. While traditionally aid was seen as a transfer of resources from rich countries to poor ones and as a way to undertake individual construction projects and other specific tasks, increasingly it is seen as a means to improve the use of domestic resources in the host countries and to expand the overall volume of those resources.[8] The slogan that became prevalent in the development community as a means to justify continued aid—"aid is trade"—is telling. This shift resulted in a change in the nature of aid: from specific development-related projects in sectors such as health, education, and agriculture to aid aimed at encouraging the adoption of growth-oriented macroeconomic policies and supporting institutions.

This shift, also described as a change from so-called project lending to program lending, brought the issue of aid conditionality to the fore. While it is usually not very difficult to convince governments to implement specific projects in the health or agriculture sectors, particularly when the bulk of the resources was provided by donors, convincing them to implement a new macroeconomic framework including difficult fiscal adjustments is much more difficult. The politically unpopular costs of these policies are visible a priori, while the benefits of sustained growth tend to become visible only in the medium or long term. This creates a "principal agent" problem, as governments often have difficulty committing to policies with direct and negative political effects that are (obviously) not shared by the donors.

Doubts among donors about recipient government commitment, meanwhile, have led to an increasing focus on conditionality. The average number of conditions placed on multilateral development bank loans actually increased throughout the 1980s.[9]

A 1991 World Bank study gave a good example of the thinking guiding conditionality efforts in the 1980s and early 1990s. It argued that aid often fails, or even makes matters worse, under the following conditions or patterns of behavior:[10]

—when it allows countries to postpone needed economic reforms by continuing to provide financial resources that support or at permit the continuation of poor policies and stagnant economies;

—when it distorts internal markets, for example by flooding recipients' food markets in a way that depresses prices unrealistically and thereby hurts local farmers;

—when it is highly unpredictable and variable; and

—when recipients allow the availability of external advice to substitute for efforts to develop the internal institutions that are necessary for long-term economic and social development.

By contrast, there are clear conditions under which aid can be quite helpful to a recipient:

—when its availability is predicated on the continuation of healthy economic policies, thereby improving the prospects that those policies will be sustained and providing incentives for countries with poor policies to carry out reforms;

—when it invests in long-term projects to develop infrastructure, human capital, and other resources that the private sector, with its near-term to medium-term time horizon, tends to underfund; and

—when it is accompanied by competent technical advice, be it on agricultural policy or health care or environmental protection or the proper functioning of governmental and legal institutions.

But even as the emphasis on conditionality increased, the effectiveness of that approach was increasingly called into doubt. One problem is enforceability. While compliance with some conditions, such as the stabilization of inflation or the devaluation of the exchange rate, is easily measurable, others, such as progress in reforming the tax system or in improving civil service performance, are much more difficult to evaluate and therefore to enforce. Another problem is that of fungibility. With project aid, support for immunizations or for an irrigation project, for example, is difficult to divert to other purposes. Yet the general balance of payments support provided by program aid can be used by governments in a variety of different ways, many of which run counter to the objectives of growth-oriented reform (such as maintaining an excessive public sector wage bill).

The debate on aid effectiveness and conditionality was heightened in the 1990s with the publication of a number of studies—several of them originating in the multilaterals themselves—that found little positive relationship between conditioned financial aid flows and economic growth. Indeed, the majority even found this relationship to be on balance negative, particularly in low-income countries and in Africa.[11] Yet these same studies acknowledged that the broader policy orientation that program aid seeks to promote—market-friendly, open economic policies with a prudent approach to macro management—is producing strong results worldwide. While some countries have adopted market-oriented policies, many with little or no external aid, and have had strong growth performance as a result, others, particularly low-income countries in Africa, failed to adopt those policies despite increasing levels of program-related conditional aid.

This record raises several issues. First, has aid truly been that ineffective, or would the poorly performing countries have fared even worse in the absence of aid? Second, how effective is conditionality in its current form, and should it be reconceptualized? Third, what is the causal relationship underlying this record: do the policies produce poor growth results, or do the poor human and economic conditions now prevailing in most major aid recipients prevent the implementation of policies that in turn enhance growth?

This latter point has obvious implications for the design of aid. In poor performing low-income countries, should it focus on improving initial human and social conditions without aspiring to see progress on the macroeconomic front right away, as it did in the 1960s and 1970s, or should it continue to promote the implementation of the policies that have proven successful in promoting growth in other countries?

Does Aid Tend to Lead to Economic Growth?

One of the most paradoxical findings of recent studies of aid effectiveness is that, at least in the case of conditioned policy-based lending, financial flows are negatively correlated with growth performance. That is, countries getting more aid do worse macroeconomically, on average, than those getting less.

Aid's record is much better when appropriate policies are in place. One study, which also found that *on average* aid had no effects on growth, found that aid did increase the growth rates in those countries with "good policies" (open trading regimes, low inflation, and small budget deficit). Yet performance rarely determines how aid is allocated: the tendency for aid to reward good policies has been overwhelmed by donors' pursuit of their own strategic interests. (Multilateral aid does slightly better than bilateral aid in rewarding good policies.)[12]

If one merely looks at average ratios of aid to GNP worldwide, the negative relationship between aid flows and performance is clear at a general level: African nations have an aid-to-GNP ratio that is more than five times that of either Latin America or East Asia (see figure 2-9 on foreign aid per capita, per region), but markedly inferior economic performance.[13] More detailed empirical studies, based on regression analysis, confirm this general trend. In their 1991 study, Paul Mosley, Jane Harrigan, and John Toye, using a sample of twenty low- and middle-income countries, found a negative effect of World Bank financial flows on growth performance (defined as GDP growth, export growth, import growth, and investment as a share of GDP).[14] In contrast, the effects of compliance with Bank policy conditions had a strong, positive, and statistically significant effect on export and GNP growth rates for the same sample of countries, although the response was (not surprisingly) lagged.[15] Other studies, which use broader measures of aid flows, find that on average aid has no effects on growth, positive or negative.[16]

A comparison of countries with and without structural adjustment loans—that is, conditional program lending from the World Bank intended to help a country make the transition to growth-oriented macroeconomic policies—found that a majority of adjustment loan recipients had better trade performance than non-loan recipients, despite receiving less aid per capita. It also found, however, that they had worse government investment performance and little difference from other countries in growth rates.[17] "The strong, immediate negative response of exports to Bank finance is a surprising response, which reinforces the view that the disbursement of programme aid finance, by reducing the immediate pressure to adjust to a balance of payments financing gap, may retard the recipient's pace of adjustment, hence resulting in a negative impact on variables such as GDP and export growth rates in the short term."[18]

This suggests that by removing a hard budget constraint, aid inflows can ease the pressure to change failed policies and thereby impede the formation of domestic consensus on the need for difficult economic adjustments. Recent research at the World Bank comes to a similar conclusion, albeit in a different manner. Using a sample of fifty-five developing countries that had rescheduled external debt, Michael Bruno and William Easterly show that those with consistently moderate levels of inflation grew more slowly over a period of time than those that entered serious inflation crises (with annual rates over 40 percent) at some point.[19]

Rather ironically, inflation crises often had the positive effect of forcing a domestic consensus in favor of the reforms necessary to halt high or hyper inflation. This consensus often gave governments the political opportunity to go beyond stabilization and implement both macroeconomic and institutional reforms (such as trade liberalization, pension reform, and the introduction of independent central banks)—reforms that are essential to sustained growth.[20] Countries with lower inflation were able to muddle along with mediocre policies and at much slower rates of growth. Aid flows tended to reinforce this trend: they continued to the countries with moderate rates of inflation, but usually stopped when severe crisis hit (aid tended to drop when the inflation rate reached 150–200 percent).[21]

The importance of a country's forming a consensus in favor of reform cannot be stressed enough. A recent World Bank study, for example, which reviewed eighty-one adjustment loan operations, found that thirty-six of these (44 percent) had satisfactory economic performance outcomes and were associated with a high degree of borrower support for reform, sometimes called borrower "ownership." Twenty-three others (28 percent) had unsatisfactory performance outcomes that corresponded to low borrower ownership.[22] The factors that were associated with a high degree of ownership were: political stability; support of (or lack of opposition from) various constituencies; and, to a lesser extent, preconceived official attitudes for or against certain kinds of reform. Ownership was *not* determined by the nature of the political regime; external or exogenous shocks; initial conditions; and/or the nature of government-Bank interaction.[23]

This obviously raises questions about the role of aid flows, and in particular of conditionality, in supporting or preventing the development of such a consensus, and about why such consensus develops in some countries and not in others. The experience of extreme crisis, which forces reforms because of the widespread acceptance that there is no alternative and that the solution is not going to come from abroad, is part of the answer.

Yet even if the effects are often positive in the long run, allowing countries to enter deep crises before undertaking reform hardly seems an acceptable policy approach. Deep crises have major social costs, and not all of them are resolved peacefully. Moreover, in some contexts, aid has played an important role in the development of a consensus in favor of reform. In Poland in 1989, external support was a critical benefit that the reform team could deliver and was therefore key to its political ascent. In other countries, such as Chile, the role of aid was neutral, and reforms were driven by strong consensus among a core group of policymakers.[24]

There is a wide debate about the timing and role of aid flows in relation to reform, much of it beyond the scope of this study. What is clear is that aid flows to countries lacking a consensus in favor of reform have a negative effect. Why has so much aid continued to flow even when not tied to reform efforts?

Reevaluating Conditionality

Conditionality, as used here, implies a contract between a donor and a borrower in which the borrower must meet certain conditions in order to receive and have continued access to loans. Most conditionality programs are run by multilateral institutions such as the IMF and the World Bank, which act as "lender of last resort" and provide credit at lower than market rates.[25] Conditionality is usually applied "ex ante," that is borrowing countries must meet certain conditions in order to be eligible for a loan and then continue to meet other conditions in order to have subsequent tranches of the loan disbursed.

Despite a marked increase in conditional lending in the 1980s, there is increasing consensus that conditionality has had limited success, as is evidenced in the discussion above. Indeed, there may even be a negative cycle: since borrower "ownership" of policy reforms is often low and donor confidence that conditions will be completed weak, more and more conditions have been applied to loans. The higher the number of conditions, the more likely governments will see them as externally imposed encumbrances and the greater the incentive to avoid full compliance. A high number of technical conditions can also be very difficult to comply with, particularly if a country experiences unexpected political developments or exogenous economic shocks.

Incentives on the donor side, meanwhile, often reward the continuation of lending rather than the halting of financial flows in response to breaches in compliance. The World Bank, for example, is at its core a lending institution. Thus from an internal institutional point of view, an average loan officer there often feels greater pressure to fully disburse approved loans than to enforce strict compliance with conditions in the recipient countries. In addition, in the 1980s, wide exposure to a number of highly indebted countries resulted in the Bank's having a strong stake in continued lending to prevent those nations' insolvency.[26]

Moreover, after several years or a decade of receiving adjustment loans, many African nations and some others have accumulated sizable debts to the IMF and World Bank. Ironically, financial exposure may place more pressure on the Bretton Woods agencies to make new loans than on recipient nations to carry out the conditions attached to the loans. If governments believe that they will continue to receive significant flows of nonproject aid with only soft conditions attached, pressure to take painful adjustment measures is eased considerably.[27]

By the Bank's own calculations, only 60 percent of agreed conditions are fully implemented during a loan period, yet in almost every case, release of the second tranche of the loan is eventually approved.[28] A number of the countries that have the worst records of complying with conditions, including Kenya, Ecuador, and the Philippines (before 1985), have received followup program finance from the Bank with relative ease—a fact clearly noted by other borrowers from the Bank that has, not surprisingly, contributed to broader noncompliance.[29]

Two additional elements contribute to the complexity of the conditionality issue. These are enforceability and fungibility. As mentioned above, some conditions are much easier to enforce than others. It is relatively easy to verify whether a finance ministry has devalued the currency or stabilized inflation. Conditionality is most effective and easiest to enforce when measures can be readily monitored; when they can be put into effect by a small number of actors rather than requiring extensive institutional change or the cooperation of multiple agencies; when they can be accomplished in a single step; when they create opportunities for further reforms or new private sector activity; and when a strong technical consensus supports them.[30] Yet many reforms that are critical to structural adjustment do not fit these categorizations. Policy measures that require a larger number of actors, such as increasing tax collections or reforming the civil service, are much more complex and difficult to enforce than those that meet the above criteria.

Fungibility is an issue that applies primarily to policy-based rather than project lending. Unlike project loans, which are tied to specific sectors and locations, policy-based loans are essentially lump sums of money designed to support the balance of payments. It is therefore very difficult to ensure that the money is not used for purposes that run counter to the reform objectives that the loans are intended to support—for example, that balance of payments support is not used to maintain an oversized public sector.

Despite these problems associated with enforcement, conditionality also plays three important and positive roles that extend beyond the issues of enforcement and fungibility. It is a means for the government to send out positive signs to the private sector. Conversely, at times it serves as a rating mechanism for private agents such as investors. Finally, it can serve as a convenient source of blame for unpopular policies, thus potentially alleviating some of the political pressure on governments.

Yet the combination of factors contributing to the difficulty of enforcing conditionality, and therefore to its lack of effectiveness, has led to a debate about its modality. Numerous observers, and even some World Bank reports, have called for a reevaluation of conditionality, aiming toward more selectivity in lending, fewer conditions and increased domestic involvement in the design of programs, and stricter enforcement when conditions are not met. For conditionality to be credible, enforcement must be applied strictly across the board—which is far from current practice.[31] At the least, multilaterals should cease to lend when blatant slippage on major conditions occurs.

A more fundamental shift in lending practices would be to use ex post instead of ex ante conditionality. Instead of applying a high number of detailed conditions, donors and borrowers would agree on a policy package, and the borrower's eligibility for future loans would depend on applying the package within an agreed period of time. In this manner, disagreements over specific measures would be avoided, and the focus of attention would be the general approach to policy. Such an approach would be far more likely to encourage "ownership" of policy reforms, as the specific measures entailed would not be seen as "imposed" from abroad. This approach would not be appropriate for countries without experience in designing sound economic policies or an established track record with the multilateral financial institutions. In these cases, at least some ex ante conditionality would be necessary.

While a shift toward more selective lending based on ex post conditionality makes a good deal of intuitive sense, it also entails substantial risk. It could result in the withdrawal of funds from many poor, low-income countries, particularly in Africa. Given the track record of lending to these countries thus far, a withdrawal of financial flows may be an effective means of generating a shift to genuine policy reforms in some.

Yet there are also likely to be some dramatic failures, where aid is withdrawn and governments do not adopt the necessary reforms and performance deteriorates even further. These failures will have high social costs. At the least, such costs should be mitigated with continued flows of humanitarian aid, coupled with unconditional technical assistance to either government or nongovernment actors depending on the attitude of the government.

The same evidence that demonstrates a mixed result for financial flows related to aid also suggests that the most important contribution of aid is the influence of ideas: when these ideas are internalized by a critical mass within societies, reforms are then "owned" and successfully implemented. The experience of many east Asian countries in the 1970s and then Latin American countries in the 1980s and 1990s supports this proposition. Greater selectivity in the provision of resources, particularly fungible ones such as balance of payments support, would probably increase the effectiveness of aid by forcing more countries to address the issue of economic reform head on.

Using greater selectivity in the manner in which aid is allocated could help cope with the cuts in aid resources that have taken place in the United States and in many other donor states during this decade (and which seem likely to continue in the short term at least). Although in this study we call for more aid resources, we also recognize that as a practical matter real budgets may continue to decline. Selectivity can help ensure that whatever resources are available are used to maximum benefit.

Finally, such a strategy might alleviate some of the current public skepticism about aid and thereby help arrest the downward trends in available resources. More effective aid is obviously more likely to sustain support. It is also more likely to sustain enthusiasm among aid practitioners, whose own morale is being tested by the vocal political opposition to foreign assistance in the U.S. Congress and by the new questions that are being raised about the effectiveness of aid among practitioners themselves.

The Chicken or the Egg: Do Policies or Initial Conditions Determine Economic Performance?

In advocating a fundamental shift in the manner in which we view and allocate aid, it is important to consider the question of whether countries are poor and perform poorly on the macroeconomic front because of their initial conditions, such as per capita income levels and natural resource endowments, or because they pursue inappropriate policies over time.

In a recent comparative study, Jeffrey Sachs and Andrew Warner tested the so-called convergence theory of economic growth, which posits that poor countries grow faster than wealthier ones because they enjoy a higher rate of return to capital investment. This eventually leads to a convergence of income levels.[32] Some worldwide trends seem to dispute this theory: from 1970 to 1989, many poor countries, particularly in sub-Saharan Africa, not only failed to grow faster than rich ones, but experienced negative per capita growth. As a consequence the gap between their income levels and those of the richest countries widened significantly. This record led to theories of a "convergence club": only countries with an adequate level of human capital endowments can take advantage of modern technology to enjoy the possibility of convergent growth. A related theory also emerged: that poor countries have low long-term potential, though countries do tend to grow faster in the early stages, when the gap between their current income and their own long-term potential is greatest. All of these theories suggest that initial conditions predetermine poor countries' performance, a pessimistic scenario for poor countries and for the potential effectiveness of aid.

Sachs and Warner dispute this theory, arguing that policies rather than initial conditions matter most. Those countries that manage their economies poorly by, for example, failing to secure property rights, following autarkic trade policies, and maintaining inconvertible currencies, are unlikely to experience convergence regardless of the underlying production technology or initial endowments of human capital. In a study of 117 countries,[33] they found that those countries that followed standard market-based policies exhibited an overwhelming tendency toward convergence, even countries that start with extremely low levels of human capital endowments and initial levels of per capita income. The authors found it difficult to identify a single case in which a poor country actually protected private property rights and maintained economic openness, and yet failed to achieve economic growth.[34]

In those countries that maintained distorting economic policies, the most damaging of these were taxes on foreign trade (such as quotas), as these not only skew incentives, but limit countries' access to international flows of knowledge. Meanwhile, very few of the countries that pursued poor policies grew at equivalent rates and in a sustainable manner, although there were a few exceptions.[35]

These results suggest that good policies are the most important variable explaining performance and that aid strategies should aim to support the adoption of such policies. While the shift to policy-based lending in the 1980s was intended to do precisely that, the manner in which it was implemented clearly did not meet those objectives and at times even impeded them. Understanding how and why aid flows failed is critical to the debate over aid.

Understanding how and when aid can *succeed* in encouraging the adoption of growth-oriented policies is equally important to the debate and arguably is an area that we know less about.[36] Properly timed aid flows can be critical to reformers, from both macroeconomic political perspectives, as the case of Poland demonstrates.

Some issues remain outstanding. For example, it is not clear whether countries adopt poor policies precisely because they are poor, which usually also implies lower levels of human capital and administrative skills, or if the poor policies were in place over a long period of time and resulted in increased poverty. In the case of Korea, for example, it is not clear to what extent liberalization resulted in economic growth and to what extent economic growth resulted in the political conditions that made liberalization possible.[37] These were most likely mutually reinforcing phenomena, a dynamic in which external aid played a supporting role. In Poland in 1989, meanwhile, access to external resources was one appeal of the reformist camp. It helped make their election possible, leading to the implementation of reforms under extremely difficult "initial conditions." In most low-growth, low-income countries, poor policies have been in place for decades. In such countries, where political or institutional conditions are often not conducive to the implementation of appropriate policies, external support has an obvious role in encouraging change.

Implications for Future Assistance

"Many economists now argue that the combination of debt forgiveness and the knowledge that new finance will have to be found by attracting private capital or by encouraging the return of private flight capital, would do more for economic reform than donor consultative group meetings and endless donor cajolery and threats."[38]

This by no means suggests a drastic curtailment of overall aid levels; indeed the level of cuts in aid that are currently proposed could potentially be quite damaging to U.S. capacity to aid effectively. In many cases, it is the promise of future assistance—for example when it is withheld—that forces a new consensus on policy reform. Rewarding success cases is extremely important to encouraging poor performers to adopt appropriate policies. It can also produce results: for example, David Dollar and Craig Burnside estimate that the same amount of aid, allocated on the basis of policy rather than donor interest, would raise the mean growth rate in their sample of poor countries from 1.10 percent to 1.44 percent. Rewards should come not only in the form of aid flows, but in the form of debt forgiveness, open markets for trade, and new private capital inflows. Official flows can serve as an important bridge to achieving these rewards once reforms have been adopted—for example, by boosting investor confidence in a previously high risk country. A realistic level of resources will remain necessary to encourage governments to work toward those goals as well as to help them cover transition costs along the way.[39] Determining what this level might be is the subject of the remaining chapters.

4

Budgetary Implications of Aid Selectivity

*T*HIS CHAPTER translates the assessment of aid effectiveness in chapter 3 into a specific budgetary framework. In particular, it estimates the magnitude of aid resources that should be offered or provided to reforming countries and the much smaller amounts that might be given to those that do not adopt sound economic practices and policies.

Today, per capita aid levels are more a function of a recipient's wealth, geographic location, and size than of its policies. Among poor states that fail to attract much private capital or otherwise show immediate economic promise, smaller countries and those in Africa, the Middle East, and the Central America–Caribbean region tend to receive the most external assistance, often obtaining $30 or more per person annually. Larger poor countries and those in South Asia do worst, typically being provided less than $10 per person per year and in some cases less than $5.

The chief argument of this study, translated into specific dollar terms below, is that this somewhat accidental and economically unsound global aid situation should be changed. On average, truly poor countries should receive resources at about the level of $15 per person for basic human and humanitarian needs such as population planning and child survival. In such cases, those efforts should involve a direct donor role in carrying out projects on the ground. But only countries that have adopted or are trying to adopt good macroeconomic policies should generally receive large sums beyond that base.

Aid for Grass-Roots and Humanitarian Purposes

How much aid money is used for basic grass-roots activities and needs? It can make a difference in people's lives and help contain global population growth and environmental destruction even when governments follow poor policies, and it should generally be continued or augmented. And how much is devoted to infrastructural development, debt relief, balance of payments support, and nationwide programs in education, health, and other areas? The latter efforts can only be expected to bear fruit if private markets are functioning well and recipient governments are performing competently and within their means.

To answer this question, consider the main categories of the Organization for Economic Cooperation and Development (see figure 2-11). They are social programs of various sorts including health care and education; administrative and institutional improvements; agricultural development; industrial development; and loans. Together they account for about 90 percent of all aid. (Food aid constitutes an additional 2 to 3 percent of total assistance, and administrative overhead another 8 to 10 percent.) Funding for basic human needs and grass-roots efforts is found in agricultural assistance as well as some social programs in health, types of aid that do not generally require major capital investment or highly effective central government direction and oversight. These categories represent roughly one-third of the dollar total. So as a rough approximation, some $20 billion of the roughly $60 billion global aid effort should probably not be affected by any conditionality policy.[1] Because most of that $20 billion is devoted to the 2 billion or so people living in Africa, the Middle East, parts of Latin America, and most of south Asia, one can think of this assistance in per capita terms as about $10 a person a year.

There are good reasons to think this amount insufficient, however. Organizations such as UNICEF, the World Bank, and nongovernmental entities have estimated that resources and technical assistance to developing countries for such purposes should probably be expanded substantially. Generally, increases on the order of 50 percent would be needed to reach all populations adequately.

That amount comes from estimating the percent of a population covered by existing programs in the above areas. Presumably, then, the remaining target population could be covered at roughly the same per capita expense. In addition, donors would provide the same fractional share of funding—generally one-fourth to one-third of the total—as in existing programs. The remainder would be left to the host nation, to ensure its full support. Recipient governments already typically spend at least 5 percent to 7 percent of their GDP on education and health and other basic human needs; doubling that commitment in countries that often can collect no more than a few percent of GDP in taxes would generally be very difficult. Yet in many countries, these expenditures are allocated to services that benefit the wealthy rather than the poor, such as higher education, and could be reallocated.[2] The net effect is that, on average, the per capita funding requirement for basic human and humanitarian needs is about $15 a year. In practical terms, the underfunding at present is probably greatest in parts of South Asia, but it exists elsewhere as well.

The other two-thirds of aid dollars, or about $40 billion a year from all donors, is more large-scale or macroeconomic in nature. These aid dollars are unlikely to contribute substantially to development in the absence of reform in the recipient countries. Dollars are likely to be wasted on oversized and inefficient bureaucracies, on import subsidies, or on infrastructure that is unlikely to be maintained—and even if maintained for a time, that is unlikely to catalyze complementary private investment because economic fundamentals are not sufficiently attractive or stable.[3] Reducing the amounts of aid in these categories that is given to countries with poor economic policies can save substantial amounts of money. However, providing sufficient incentive and economic spark to reforming countries may require more resources per person than the amounts now transferred.

Aid for General Economic Development and Nationwide Programs

What funds and technical assistance and other help should be accorded countries that do have good economic policies, above and beyond the amounts they receive to support basic grass-roots and relief efforts?

There are good reasons to think these amounts should be more than is generally provided today. A good way to see this—admittedly not a definitive way of calculating any given country's specific resource needs today, but a very useful first cut at requirements from basic principles—is to examine what worked so well in the cases of the East Asian "tigers." The following section examines those two tigers that have the most diversified economies and thus should be most representative of the needs and potential of a still-developing country today.

The South Korean and Taiwanese Experiences

For countries willing to adopt and stick with realistic exchange rates and low and simple tariff regimes, reduce budget deficits, limit consumer subsidies for imported goods, improve legal systems and property rights, streamline public sectors, and otherwise pursue policies likely to lead to sustainable growth, overall aid levels would optimally be higher than they are in many cases today.

Experience suggests that development assistance is most successful when viewed as a temporary but significant instrument of policy. Aid seems most successful when it is used for a fixed period of time to support the establishment of basic education and health systems, build infrastructure, and if necessary facilitate fundamental social and economic changes (such as land reform in the cases of South Korea and Taiwan— or in today's world, transition to a market economy or demilitarization of excessively large armed forces). It seems less successful in African, South Asian, and Mideast countries that have taken a more gradual course to reform and development supported by moderately large levels of aid over extended periods of time.[4]

As suggested, the analysis builds heavily on the cases of South Korea and Taiwan in the 1950s and 1960s. It would be less appropriate to focus on the Marshall Plan states of Europe and Japan since they were effectively rebuilding infrastructure and industry that they had once possessed. It would also be less appropriate to try generalizing from the cases of Singapore and Hong Kong, city states with very specific geographic and demographic characteristics. In the 1960s and 1970s South Korea and Taiwan each grew at about 9 percent a year on average, or some 7 percent in real per capita terms.[5]

It is also most helpful to focus on economic assistance. Even though military aid may allow a recipient to devote more of its own resources to economic matters, everything else being equal, a country's actual military requirements are highly dependent on its specific security situation. Moreover, even if onerous, those military requirements do not necessarily handicap a country economically, as the cases of South Korea, Israel, and Taiwan demonstrate.[6]

In the 1950s the United States—effectively South Korea's only major aid provider—gave that country an average of roughly $1.5 billion a year (expressed in 1997 dollars) in economic and development assistance.[7] The economic aid was comparable in size to the country's total imports and was about 10 percent the size of its GDP. On a per capita basis, it corresponded to roughly $65 annually, given the country's population of roughly 20–25 million at that time.[8]

After 1960 economic aid to South Korea dropped off, totaling only half of its earlier value by the early 1970s and then effectively ending in the next few years. Aid to Taiwan followed a similar pattern, reaching a level of roughly $500 million a year (again, in constant 1997 dollars) in the late 1940s and remaining there for about a decade before falling off by half in the early 1960s and essentially ending by the late 1960s. At its peak, aid represented some 5 percent of GDP on average. On a per capita basis, it totaled about $50 a year.[9]

Another way to view these numbers is to observe that the flow of aid to each country over the fifteen to twenty years of intensive assistance programs wound up totaling on the order of $1,000 per person (1997 dollars). Countries that remain mired in poverty and aid dependency for three or four or five decades, receiving some $30 per year per person over that stretch, thus have received as many resources in the aggregate as did South Korea and Taiwan yet have far less to show for them.

It would be a mistake to assume that one could immediately transfer the experiences of South Korea and Taiwan to other developing countries. Notably, the amount of influence that the United States had over those countries, dependent as they were on Washington for help in the security realm, is difficult to equal when many more donors are involved and recipients are more protective of their own decisionmaking rights. And without the host country's commitment to sound policies, no amount of aid will make a fundamental difference. Yet precisely because of that, the purpose of a more effective—and selective—aid strategy is to try to recapture some of the clarity and efficiency of earlier aid efforts and to encourage economic reform above all else.

Lessons for Development Today

Of course, the development experience of all other developing countries cannot be expected to mirror those of the two cases considered above. Taiwan and South Korea had their own historical and cultural attributes that do not resemble those of many other states. But they can provide a good model for other developing countries. The point is that certain economic and governmental fundamentals are essentially prerequisites to growth, and that South Korea and Taiwan focused squarely on those fundamentals. To put it differently and in the language of chapter 3, their success is explained less by initial conditions than by specific policies. Even if initial conditions facilitated the adoption of certain policies, it is the policies that should be viewed as the chief explanatory variable. With that in mind, one can generalize from the South Korean and Taiwanese experiences to estimate desirable global aid levels from first principles.

The aid figures for Taiwan and South Korea—roughly $50 to $65 per person per year, or 5 to 10 percent of recipient GDP—contrast with today's average of about $25 per capita worldwide in poorer developing countries.[10] In the case of South Korea, however, some of the aid in earlier periods was devoted to immediate recovery from war. So the range of annual funds for economic development might be viewed as $50 to $60 per person.

The per person measure is not the only one to consider, however. Specifically, some developing countries may already be near their capacity to absorb aid. Poorer countries with weak institutions and relatively poorly trained work forces are less well positioned to undertake large-scale and capital intensive projects than are wealthier states. The poorest countries of the world tend to have per capita GDPs ranging from roughly $200 to $700. Thus in some of those cpuntries aid as a percentage of GDP is already about 5 to 10 percent. These figures compare relatively favorably with those of Taiwan and South Korea in the 1950s and 1960s.[11]

What is more, rapid expansion of aid levels in the interest of making macroeconomic spreadsheets look good would risk repeating the mistakes of earlier eras of development. As we know now, achieving a given level of investment is no guarantee of sustainable growth. Funds can be misspent on "white elephant" projects, infrastructure that is not maintained after being built, or industries in which a given economy does not enjoy a comparative advantage.

Recipient countries have often had a bias in favor of such projects. Their tendency was reinforced by a similar bias among a number of donor organizations such as the World Bank, in part because they could most easily measure the local effects of infrastructural or industrial development—and sometimes confused isolated success stories with broader improvement of an economy.[12] Today there is far more emphasis on appropriate policies and programs, rather than on isolated projects, among donors and many recipients. But good policies are still sometimes accepted in theory, yet diluted or ignored in practice.

Considering these various measures as a whole, the weight of evidence suggests that today's least developed countries can benefit in most cases from more aid, provided they are reforming their economies and are committed to use the resources professionally and seriously. In some cases current aid levels could be doubled. In other cases more modest funding increases would be more prudent and more likely to generate sound results. On the whole, counting grass-roots and humanitarian programs as well as programs tailored to broader economic development, reforming countries might benefit from per capita annual aid levels of roughly $35 to $60.

Debt Relief

Some funds above and beyond those estimated above may also be needed to service external debts. Sums owed to public organizations are already accounted for in the above analysis, if one simply interprets aid requirements as net rather than as gross amounts (and ODA figures, including those in this study, are generally in terms of net disbursements). But debts owed to private creditors and to public organizations like the International Monetary Fund (IMF) that are not, strictly speaking, providers of aid may lead to additional resource requirements.

Consider the sub-Saharan Africa and South Asia regions. Each pays out about $2 billion a year to the World Bank, $3 billion to $5 billion annually to private creditors, and about $2 billion in repayments to the IMF. This suggests that countries need on average about $10 per person a year to service their non-ODA debts. Donors need not feel obliged to provide this funding in all cases by any means—there is, after all, no guarantee that some countries will not simply develop new debt obligations. But in calculating total resource flows to reformist countries, they need to keep in mind this significant element that does not show up in ODA calculations. When implementing debt relief in the future, moreover, they may be as wise to help with annual service payments—and thereby retain leverage over recipients to keep their policies in good shape—as to provide one-time debt forgiveness. (The latter approach was taken in the September 1996 Paris Club package that, after a "waiting period," will provide about $8 billion in forgiveness for twenty of the world's most heavily indebted poor countries.)[13]

The existence of these debt obligations also suggests that one should not be too optimistic about the potential savings from a more selective aid strategy. Many of the countries that are pursuing poor policies and would theoretically be cut off from aid for economic development are currently using a substantial part of those aid flows to repay both public and private debt. Cutting off some recipient countries would entail a net loss for the international financial institutions in the short term unless aid dollars were used to reimburse them.[14]

Because of such constraints, even African countries that have adopted sound economic policies are still underinvesting in their economies' long-term capital bases. Most successful developing countries have devoted about 25 percent of their GDP to investment during periods of growth, but African countries remain stuck in the range of roughly 15 to 20 percent. By helping them and perhaps some South Asian and Middle Eastern countries with their private debt, at the cost of roughly $10 per person per year, donors could substantially enhance the prospects for reform and sustainable growth in those countries. Selectivity is critical with debt relief, as it is with aid, however; relief should only be provided to those countries that are pursuing sound macroeconomic policies.

Reconstructing Societies Ravaged by Conflict

What if any additional resources might be required to help countries that have been held down or set back by prolonged political or military conflict?

In many ways, rebuilding a war-torn country tends to be like development in a poor country, particularly if the country at issue was relatively nonindustrialized to begin with and has a population with rather limited educational attainments and economic skills. South Korea's development experience illustrates this relationship. South Korea's initial postwar aid benefits of about $65 per person per year were quite high, but not much higher than Taiwan's level of about $50 and only slightly higher than they remained even into the 1960s, when the immediate consequences of the civil war were already alleviated.

The situation could be somewhat different in a country that had been industrialized before war and was then in need of massive repair rather than development per se. The Marshall Plan provided aid of $40 billion to $50 billion a year for about three years to several hundred million people, meaning that aid levels were well in excess of $100 per person annually and in some cases $200 or more. But the duration of the aid programs was short, so the aggregate aid per recipient—on the order of

$500 to $1,000—is similar to that of the smaller but much longer aid programs for South Korea and Taiwan. It is also comparable to the amounts spent in many countries that have remained poor since the advent of the development assistance era some four decades ago.[15]

Also, certain aid needs are clearly specific to societies coming out of protracted periods of crisis or conflict. In addition to emergency humanitarian requirements, they can include mine clearing, employment programs designed specifically for demobilizing soldiers, efforts to build new and professional security institutions, and related matters.[16]

To understand how this applies to a specific country, consider the assistance program for the 2.2 million Palestinians in the West Bank and Gaza. The international community is spending roughly $400 million a year, or almost $200 per person, in those entities, despite the absence of major physical damage normally associated with war. The aid level is expected to rise a bit more during the five-year duration of the project. The U.S. share, consisting of bilateral programs as well as contributions to the efforts of the international financial institutions, is about one-sixth of the total, or about $500 million over five years.

Spending is broad based and oriented toward physical and human investment. Roughly 10 percent of the funds are for housing; 10 percent for health and education; 30 percent for water, sewers, and power; 15 percent for transport and telecommunications; 10 percent for industry and agriculture; and 25 percent for central direction, institution building, and feasibility and follow-up studies.[17]

At the rate of $200 per person a year, a five-year program would look fairly similar to European reconstruction efforts in the Marshall Plan years. Although this does not seem unreasonable in terms of aggregate resource flows, it is doubtful whether the nonindustrialized West Bank and Gaza Strip can productively absorb resources in the way that England and Germany and France did in the late 1940s and early 1950s. The longer-term and less expensive Taiwanese and South Korean programs, in which average annual aid per capita was typically $50 to $65 as measured in 1997 dollars, would appear on the surface to be more promising approaches for the Palestinians. The perceived political imperative for rapid economic progress, together with donors' tendency to use expensive outside contractors, may have outweighed the dictates of sound development planning in this case—although that is not to say that the effort will fail, only that it may be somewhat overambitious and inefficient.

The focus on major infrastructure projects is cause for concern, however. Since the late 1970s, most major development institutions such as the World Bank have largely shifted away from their earlier focus on such projects, recognizing that in isolation they rarely generate sustainable development. They are now trying instead to emphasize and assist with the adoption of growth-oriented macroeconomic policies and to target investments in infrastructure more carefully.[18]

International contributions to Bosnian reconstruction are even larger than those to the West Bank and Gaza Strip. The United States and other donors are providing roughly $1.25 billion a year for about 4 million people, an average of $300 per capita per year.[19] The Marshall Plan experience may be more relevant here, since this effort is partly one of reconstruction rather than crash development, and so the prognosis for Bosnia's being able to usefully absorb a given flow of funds seems better than for the West Bank and Gaza. But this program, even larger than that for the Palestinians, also appears quite ambitious—perhaps unrealistically so. It is beyond the scope of this study to determine conclusively if the resource levels are excessive, but it does seem appropriate to raise a cautionary flag.

The allocation of resources for different program and project areas is not unlike that in the West Bank and Gaza, but with more emphasis on transport and telecommunications and less on institution building. Specifically, 10 percent of the funds are intended for housing, 15 percent for health and education, 25 percent for water and sewage and power, 25 percent for transport and telecommunications, 15 percent for industry and agriculture, 5 percent for central direction and institution building, and about 5 percent for land-mine clearing. Jump-starting heavy infrastructure development in the areas of energy, transport, and water and sewage drove up the first-year price tag for 1996 to $1.8 billion.[20]

Even if such assistance packages have their potential downsides and inefficiencies, we believe firmly that the international community has no choice but to stay involved in them in the future. Without assertive and wide-reaching aid programs, the chances of a resumption of conflict appear intolerably high.

Environmental Programs

Additional funds may be needed for prudent investments to protect the global environment as well as the local environments near a number of cities and other places of special concern in developing countries. But corresponding resource requirements are unlikely to be large. The environment can best be protected by old-fashioned development: controlling population growth and promoting sustainable agriculture and related economic activities. In that sense, it is best viewed as an integral concern of basic development and not likely to pose large additional demands in its own right. However, even in the absence of a large-scale effort to reduce global warming or to address some other potentially serious problem (as could conceivably be necessary, and might well be very expensive), some special needs merit attention and modest levels of external resources.

A recent major World Bank study on long-term global environmental trends developed an illustrative agenda for action costing donors and recipients together about $70 billion a year. Nearly two-thirds of the dollars would have been devoted to the above-mentioned realms of family planning, health, education, and agriculture, as well as the related areas of forest and soil conservation. The remaining funds, about $25 billion, would have been devoted chiefly to controlling emissions from vehicles, industries, and power stations.

If donors are assumed to provide one-quarter to one-third of the necessary funding, environmental concerns might add another $6 billion to $9 billion a year to aid budgets. These figures translate into per capita annual totals of less than $5.

Moreover, conditionality can properly be applied to such assistance, and money given only to countries with sound overall policies.[21] Since local air and water pollution, regrettable as they may be, are of less importance for the planet's long-term livability than basic demographic and agricultural trends, applying the conditionality concept in this way is acceptable even if that means allowing some problems to fester for the time being.

Another category of environmental programs would cost even less. The global environment facility, set up in 1990 and reinvigorated by the Rio summit of 1992, provided $300 million a year in 1990–93 for four main objectives: maintenance of biodiversity, control of global warming, limits on ozone depletion, and protection of international waters. Proposals to expand the scale of effort were in the range of $1 billion a year from all donors combined, not appreciably affecting the above estimate of less than $5 per person per capita in targeted environmental funding.[22]

Social Safety Nets

To the extent that aid flows are increased substantially for reforming countries as we suggest, enough opportunities for employment will generally arise that special programs will not be needed to care for the most vulnerable. But if aid increases are more modest, as seems more likely, the need to target resources to the most needy is heightened.

Economic reforms generally entail reducing the size of government and parastatal payrolls and curtailing subsidies on consumer goods, including those on staple foods. These measures can be costly for certain vulnerable groups, such as the urban poor. They also tend to be strongly opposed by politically vocal groups, whose demands for government resources in compensation often compete with the needs of the poor. Effective protection of the poorest may require diverting resources from the politically vocal to needier groups.

In some contexts it has proven possible to mitigate at least the worst of such effects by programs that cost less than 1 percent of GDP and last for several years. Such programs may target nutritional assistance to the poorest, provide temporary public works projects to mitigate short-term unemployment, and support continuing efforts of local governments and nongovernmental organizations to protect the welfare of vulnerable groups.

Funds of such relatively small magnitude will rarely be sufficient to provide effective social protection on a wide scale. But large amounts of money are rarely needed. The poorest quintiles of a population generally control only a small percent of a country's GDP, often as little as 10 percent or so for the bottom 40 percent of the population. So a targeted program spending on the order of several percent of GDP—generally no more than a few tens of dollars per poor person per year in the poorest countries, or an average of less than $10 per person countrywide—would still be significant when considered in light of the relative shares of GDP held by these sectors. Such a program could provide effective protection during the most difficult period of economic adjustment. In many cases safety net efforts have had significant effects on the political sustainability of reforms at the same time.

Donors should pay only a portion of any safety net expenditures because domestic commitment is critical to the success of any social safety net effort. Given such commitment, external support for such programs can be critical, particularly in very poor countries.[23] The requisite amounts are likely to total only a few dollars per person for a fairly short time.

Summary

The South Korean and Taiwan models suggest that total economic aid in the range of $35 to $60 per person, provided over roughly a fifteen- to twenty-year period, is a wise investment. That amount can provide for basic human and humanitarian needs and help move a country toward sustainable growth. Donors have demonstrated that they may choose to provide at least twice those sums to developing countries emerging from conflict, though their basis for doing so is not entirely clear. Countries with large debts may need up to another $10 per person to ensure adequate resources for domestic purposes, however. Countries with special environmental protection or social safety–net needs may benefit greatly from targeted programs involving up to $5 per person per year from donors. These numbers together total roughly $50 to $75 per person annually in resource flows. Countries with poor policies should generally not be accorded substantially more than about $15 to $25 a person annually, though exceptions may arise.

5

Constructing an Alternative Budget for Development Aid

*H*OW DOES one proceed from the recommended per-capita aid levels discussed in chapter 4 to an estimate of a global total for official development assistance? What are the implications for U.S. aid budgets as well as for international spending overall? Although it is impossible to be precise, an illustrative calculation can be made following the broad logic of the study. The first step is to make an estimate of what fraction of countries might be deemed to have generally good economic policies and what fraction to have poor ones.

How Many Countries Should Get More Aid, and How Many, Less?

How many countries have good policies, how many have bad ones, and what number might be somewhere in between? Fortunately, defining good policies is not particularly difficult. By now there is wide agreement, both within and outside the international financial institutions, on what they are. They feature restrained fiscal and monetary policies, reasonably small public sectors, realistic exchange rates, positive real interest rates, and liberalized trading regimes.

Extensive economic data for developing countries have now been accumulated over periods spanning oil shocks, global recessions and recoveries, shifts in global trade patterns, the emergence of Asia, and other phenomena. Incorporating them all into its models, the World Bank is able to calculate that having very good economic policies will lead countries to grow at roughly 3 percent to 4 percent a year faster than they would with poor policies. By these indicators, roughly half of current

69

recipients are pursuing policies broadly consistent with long-term growth, while the other half are not.[1]

For example, in a survey of the economic policies of twenty-six sub-Saharan African states, the World Bank found that exactly half—with a combined population of 58 percent of the total sample—had good or fair economic policies in the 1990–91 period. The other half, with 41 percent of the people, had policies deemed poor or very poor. Paradoxically, the latter group received more aid in 1991—58 percent of the total, or $48 per person, in contrast to $25 per person for countries with good policies.

This comparison may overstate the paradox: if Nigeria is eliminated from the group with good or fair policies on the grounds that its extensive oil revenues make aid less relevant to its situation, the figure for aid per person rises to $44 for countries with good policies. However, that amount is still less than the level for countries with poor policies, as shown in figure 5-1.[2] Other more recent studies reach similar conclusions, showing that outwardly oriented countries, though following recommended policies, receive on average less aid relative to GNP than countries with protective policies.[3]

Consider also the overall experience of the world's thirty-six poorest countries from 1980 to 1993, and specifically those twenty-seven for which complete data sets on GNP growth are available.[4] Of the twenty-seven, sixteen countries had negative per capita GNP growth over the period at issue and eleven positive. One might expect that those with positive growth rates were also those that received more aid—but this was not the case. In fact, they received substantially less. Part of the discrepancy is caused by the larger economies in Asia, several of which did reasonably well economically with little aid during the period in question. But even if one attempts to control for historical and regional factors by comparing only the poor countries of sub-Saharan Africa, countries with positive per capita GDP growth received slightly less aid on average than those with negative growth.[5]

More formal regression analysis techniques support this general conclusion as well and also demonstrate that aid does not generally have any discernible effect on the amount of GDP a country devotes to investment.[6] It may be worth noting that the track record is not clearly better if one rejects this line of reasoning and views aid as an instrument of gaining political influence—for every South Korea there is an Iran, or a Zaire, or a Somalia, or a Sudan.

FIGURE 5-1. *Aid Levels[a] and Economic Performance in Africa, 1991*

Aid per capita in dollars

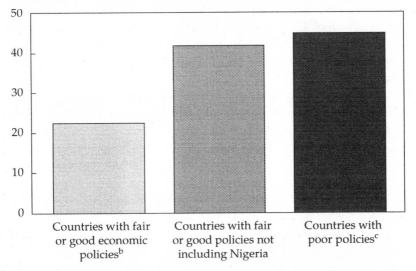

Sources: World Bank, *Adjustment in Africa* (New York: Oxford University Press, 1994), pp. 268–69; World Bank, *World Development Report 1993* (New York: Oxford University Press, 1993), pp. 238–39, 276–77.

a. Official development assistance; all sources.

b. As rated by the World Bank (including fiscal, monetary, and exchange-rate dimensions): Burkina Faso, Burundi, Gabon, The Gambia, Ghana, Madagascar, Malawi, Mali, Mauritania, Nigeria, Senegal, Togo, and Uganda.

c. As rated by the World Bank: Benin, Cameroon, Central African Republic, Congo, Côte d'Ivoire, Kenya, Mozambique, Niger, Rwanda, Sierra Leone, Tanzania, Zambia, and Zimbabwe.

The above analyses suggest that about half of the countries now receiving substantial aid have poor economic policies in place and that they receive perhaps slightly more than half of all aid dollars.

However, there are cases where it would be appropriate to give at least some aid for general economic development to a country with weak or mediocre policies. Consider for instance a situation where a new top-level leadership was trying to institute a serious reform program, but was saddled with inept or corrupt mid-level managers. The implementation of complex structural reforms, which require a fair amount of co-operation from numerous public agencies, would be difficult under such circumstances. In such circumstances, donors might wish to keep providing some aid, both to help train new managers and to support the reformist elements among the leadership.[7]

Or, to take another kind of situation, if a country seemed on the brink of civil war, aid flows might be continued for a time even in the absence of reform. For example, they could be used to prevent unemployment from worsening at a critical juncture, or to help satisfy an ethnic group that felt it had been discriminated against and needed some proof otherwise. These approaches will not always be necessary, and even when needed, will not always work. But they can be important.[8]

Finally, heavily indebted countries may not be able to service their private and public debts if they are cut off from outside help. If the choice is between allowing such countries to default and continuing to provide enough assistance to allow them to service their debt, the latter option may sometimes be desirable.

The second reason savings could be lower than initially expected is that, as donors became more selective, some potential recipients might feel stronger incentive to reform than before. But this effect is difficult to gauge, so the following calculations do not incorporate it explicitly.

Desirable Global Aid Levels

Because U.S. official development assistance now represents less than one-sixth of the global ODA total and is likely to remain a modest percent of that total, it is only sensible first to estimate aggregate aid needs from all donors and then to consider what an appropriate U.S. share might be. Without such a methodology, there is little objective basis for determining how large U.S. development aid should be.

A Ballpark Estimate

The 3.2 billion people living in the world's poorest countries can be thought of in three major groups of roughly equal size: China, the Indian subcontinent, and everyone else. How do the calculations from the previous chapter apply to each of these?

China has many alternative sources of hard currency—for example, it is currently the largest recipient of nonconcessional World Bank loans. It appears firmly embarked on a path of strong economic growth that should continue to provide it funds with which to take care of its own poor. In addition, any one of its citizens is less than half as likely to be poor, and less than one-third as likely to be extremely poor, as individuals from the Indian subcontinent or sub-Saharan Africa.[9] For those reasons China is probably not appropriately included with other poor countries, despite its low average per capita income.

Expanded aid efforts might, for example, focus on those poor countries together containing about 2 billion people, including states of the Indian subcontinent but not China. That is, aid might be concentrated on those states with roughly $200 to $700 a year in per capita income and poorly positioned to attract outside capital in the near term.

Consider first the generally small and medium-sized poor countries in Africa, the Middle East, and the Central America/Caribbean region. As a rough measure, assume that those judged (chiefly by economics staffs of the IMF and World Bank) to have good policies were provided roughly $65 per person per year. This dollar figure is based on previous aid efforts to Taiwan but adjusted slightly upward to account for the heavy debt burdens of many developing states today. Assume that those without good policies received roughly $15 a person for basic human needs (roughly what African countries get for those purposes now), together with an average of about $10 in economic aid for an annual total of $25 per capita. Today, about half the countries at issue would be expected to have poor or very poor policies and half would be expected to have good policies. The average aid level thus might be in the vicinity of $45 per person. For the 1 billion people at issue, resulting requirements would be about $45 billion (in constant 1997 dollars).

How much added aid should be offered to South Asia, and in particular to India and Pakistan? Those countries might be described as on the doorstep of the international economic system—given that they do already benefit to an extent from foreign private investment and from substantial nonconcessional public lending.[10] Moreover, given their size and their currently quite low levels of per capita aid, providing them with upward of $50 per capita in annual aid would represent a huge increase in global aid flows overnight. That does not seem politically plausible or developmentally logical. More sensible than a tenfold aid increase would be a conditional increase of up to $10 billion in economic development aid to the subcontinent. Coupled with an expanded aid effort for basic human and humanitarian needs in the region, total ODA flows to India and Pakistan could reach about $20 billion. With the $45 billion for poor countries in Africa, the Middle East, and parts of Latin America, aid would total $65 billion a year.

TABLE 5-1. *Rough Estimate of Global Aid Needs (ODA)*

Aid objective	Approximate cost (in 1997 U.S. dollars)
Basic human and humanitarian needs	$15/person × 2 billion = $30 billion
Economic aid for reformers in Africa, Mideast, Central America/Caribbean	$40/person × 0.5 billion = $20 billion
Debt relief for same reformers	$10/person × 0.5 billion = $5 billion
Economic aid for South Asia	$10/person × 1 billion = $10 billion
Economic aid for nonreformers	$10/person × 0.5 billion = $5 billion
Aid to China and middle income countries	$5 billion
Special aid to Israel, Egypt, others	$3 billion
Added conflict-resolution aid	$3 billion
Global total	$81 billion
Current (1995) global total	$62 billion
Net increase	$19 billion
U.S. share, UN dues scheme	nearly $5 billion
U.S. share, adjusted ratio[a]	$3 billion–$4 billion

Source: See text, especially chapters 4 and 5.

a. According to the normal UN dues scheme, the U.S. share of any increase in global official development assistance might be expected to represent 25 percent of the total, in keeping with the U.S. share of global GDP. The adjusted amount reflects our judgment that, by virtue of the unrivaled contribution its military forces make to global stability and thus to international trade, the United States should not be expected to pay quite a full share of any aid initiative.

Four other categories of aid would each add $2 billion to $3 billion to this figure. These categories include continued assistance to China for targeted purposes such as family planning and environmental protection; similar assistance to some middle-income countries; special programs for countries emerging from conflict; and continued aid to Israel, Egypt, and several other countries like Jordan. The total of all aid initiatives coupled with continuing worthwhile programs could approach $80 billion—or between $70 billion and $90 billion, given the unavoidable error and uncertainty in this calculation (see table 5-1 for a slightly different breakdown of the proposal).

Aid Levels and the Official UN Target under Our Proposal

If global ODA budgets increased to $80 billion a year, they would be roughly 30 percent greater than they are today. On average, each OECD country would be giving about 0.35 percent of its GDP over the next ten years, roughly the level of the period 1970–90.

By this calculation, the long-standing official UN objective that donors lift their average aid level from 0.3 percent of GDP to 0.7 percent appears quite excessive. That approach would raise total foreign aid from $62 billion (1995 aid disbursements expressed in 1997 dollars) to roughly $150 billion, seemingly more a politically generated goal than an analytically derived development requirement.[11] Indeed, there is good reason to hope that if aid levels are raised for a period of time, donors will be able to cut their aid levels well below 0.35 percent of GDP sometime after the year 2010. By that point, much of Africa, the Middle East, and South Asia should have been able to embark on the road to growth recently reached by a number of Latin American countries (if not yet that of the East Asian "tigers"), largely drawing to a close the post-colonial development effort. Other global problems may emerge by then, and a number of laggard countries—as well as acute humanitarian crises from time to time—will also probably ensure that foreign assistance survives indefinitely. But the general idea of providing economic development assistance to many tens of countries around the world could become obsolete.

The U.S. Foreign Assistance and International Affairs Budgets

If global aid budgets to poorer countries rose from roughly $62 billion to $80 billion, what might the resulting U.S. aid budget be? It does not seem fair—or politically realistic—to expect the United States to pay a full 25 percent share of that total $80 billion. It provides substantial non-ODA assistance, such as security aid to Israel and Egypt as well as military backup for some peacekeeping operations. It also spends much more on its military, both in absolute terms and as a percent of national wealth, than the other major OECD countries. Industrialized and developing countries alike benefit from the resulting international stability and peace. They also benefit from direct access to the U.S. market, which remains reasonably open to trade (though there is much room for improvement in this realm).

Since it already spends considerably more on overall foreign policy than most other western countries, it seems more reasonable to expect the United States to pay 15 to 20 percent of any increase in global aid. That might total $3 billion or somewhat more. Total U.S. ODA would go up from about $9 billion to $12 billion or $12.5 billion.

These calculations suggest that overall discretionary outlays for international programs should return to about $23 billion (in constant 1997 dollars), the 1980–95 average. This figure compares with the 1997 level of $19.6 billion. As a percent of GDP, U.S. official development assistance of $12 billion to $12.5 billion would remain near the level (0.15 percent) that characterized it in the early 1990s.

A figure in that range would be significantly above the president's projected level for 2002 of $16.8 billion, in constant 1997 dollars; it would be far above the $13 billion that would result from the Congress's budget-balancing plan. Some would say that budget pressures make such an increase implausible. But it would be quite modest, amounting to roughly 0.2 percent of the federal budget.

More to the point, the money is really needed. Unlike the situation with entitlements and even domestic discretionary spending, international affairs budgets are now lower than at virtually any point in the past twenty years (see table 5-2.) Defense too has been cut—but with good reason, given the demise of the Soviet threat. The end of the cold war confrontation may similarly have lessened some demands on international activities, particularly security aid. But new ones have developed over recent years, including increased U.S. foreign trade and travel, heightened concerns over proliferation and terrorism, international environmental and epidemiological issues, and the expanded needs associated with post-conflict reconstruction of several countries.

Other Reforms in Existing Aid Approaches

But what about the question of how well aid would be provided? This study has focused principally on flows of assistance, assuming implicitly that aid coupled with good policies on the part of recipients can achieve significant results. The record supports this claim, as discussed in chapter 3—the overriding priority is to make sure that aid is disbursed to the right countries. But other improvements in how aid is actually provided are needed as well. The most important has to do with U.S. AID and, by implication, the bilateral aid efforts of other donors as well.

Restructuring AID

As noted in chapter 2, the international donor community has become very large. A host of bilateral aid programs, about a dozen UN-related organizations, nongovernmental organizations, and regional as well as

TABLE 5-2. *The Federal Budget, 1962–2002*

Outlays, in billions of 1997 dollars

Type of spending	1962	1980	1990	1997	Pres-ident, 2002	Change, 1980 –97^c	Change, 1990 –97	Change, 1990 –02
International discretionary^a	26 (5)^b	24 (2)	23 (1.5)	19.6 (1.2)	17 (1)	–18%	–15%	–26%
National defense discretionary	248 (49)	251 (23)	358 (24)	268 (16)	242 (15)	7%	–25%	–32%
Domestic discretionary	64 (13)	240 (22)	216 (14)	263 (16)	242 (15)	10%	22%	12%
Social security	66 (13)	217 (20)	294 (20)	364 (22)	407 (24)	68%	24%	38%
Medicaid and other means-tested entitle-ments	20 (4)	84 (8)	112 (7)	202 (12)	226 (14)	140%	80%	102%
Medicare and other entitle-ments	71 (14)	225 (20)	246 (16)	326 (20)	379 (23)	45%	33%	54%
Net interest	33 (6)	98 (9)	220 (15)	247 (15)	212 (13)	152%	12%	–4%
Receipts and deposit insur-ance	–27 (–5)	–38 (–3)	23 (2)	–47 (–3)	–60 (–3)	n.a.	n.a.	n.a.

Sources: Executive Office of the President, *Budget of the United States Government, Fiscal Year 1998: Historical Tables* (February 1997), p. 109; Congressional Budget Office, *The Economic and Budget Outlook* (January 1997), p. xvi (for GDP deflators).

a. The average from 1962–1995 for international affairs spending was $20 billion, and that for national defense was $310 billion. Relative to those averages, the 2002 projection for international affairs and defense would be down 15 percent and 21 percent, respectively. The president's projections for 2002 are based on OMB economic assumptions; they would have to be lower under CBO assumptions.

b. Numbers in parentheses show spending as a percent of the federal total for that year.

c. Percentages may not add exactly to 100 because of rounding. The categories are those used in the budget enforcement act, except that receipts and deposit insurance are combined into one category for this chart.

n.a. = not applicable

global financial institutions such as the World Bank collaborate in development efforts. But they also compete, and confuse recipients' often weak bureaucracies, in many cases.

On the one hand, the donor community wields a great deal of technical expertise and professional competence. Since roughly one-fifth of all aid, or about $12 billion a year worldwide, is given in the form of technical assistance, a large cadre of individuals trained in various health, agricultural, educational, and other specialties and dedicated to helping developing countries is a tremendous global resource.[12]

On the other hand, the number of organizations running independent aid missions often exceeds 100 in any given African country, and the situation is not substantially different elsewhere. Dealing with so many important actors would pose coordination challenges to the best bureaucracy, and most developing countries do not have even good bureaucracies.[13] Donors do coordinate at some level, but they also have many interests besides maximizing efficiency. Bilateral donors in particular seek commercial markets for their home countries' goods, as well as political visibility; their aid agencies seek organizational autonomy and compete for influence, as bureaucracies can generally be expected to. Moreover, administrative costs tend to increase when more organizations are involved, since each one is likely to have its own country offices with sections devoted to project evaluation, public affairs, governmental relations, and the like. With so many actors competing for the attention of national policymakers, local institutions charged with carrying out projects may not get the attention or help they desperately need from donors and their own central governments.[14]

The successful U.S. aid efforts of the 1950s and 1960s in places such as Korea and Taiwan were generally characterized by a single large donor or at most several. And, as argued earlier, donors probably have greater impact in the realm of ideas and policies than in simply transferring resources—meaning that it may be worthwhile to have a few different voices in any policy discussion, but almost certainly it is not helpful to have a hundred. Thankfully a couple of donors and the International Monetary Fund do manage to exert leadership in some places; often, IMF-certified structural-adjustment programs are considered a precondition for bilateral aid by other donors and also catalyze private capital flows. But even so, the simple fact of needing to coordinate and monitor many tens of independent programs would strain any recipient.

A number of specific and sensible ideas for streamlining the donor network have been offered in recent years. One would change the U.S. Agency for International Development (AID) from an organization with a mission headquarters in most poor recipient countries to an agency that more frequently determined priorities and oversaw implementation of the U.S. bilateral aid effort without a substantial in-country presence. According to this model, which could be put into place gradually to avoid excessive disruptions and to test the approach, U.S. bilateral aid would be implemented largely through nongovernmental organizations, generally from the United States and recipient countries. They would receive considerably more funds and responsibilities from the U.S. government than they do today.[15] The United States in most cases would no longer attempt to involve itself directly in recipients' national economic policymaking, but rather would work within the frameworks established by the multilateral financial institutions. Sweden and Norway have already begun to move in this direction.[16]

This process would in effect reinforce the downsizing of AID that has occurred naturally as a number of countries have graduated from the ranks of aid recipients and others have had to be deemphasized because of declining bilateral aid budgets. At the end of the process, AID might have a presence in only half of the sixty to seventy countries it now plans to work in, and only twenty full-fledged missions instead of the thirty it intends (see table 5-3 for data on the existing draw-down plan).[17]

If AID were fundamentally redefined and scaled back, it should nonetheless retain the capacity to conduct up to ten conflict-resolution or reconstruction efforts at a time in places such as Bosnia, as suggested by Administrator Brian Atwood.[18] The U.S. capacity to mobilize airlift and other assets for humanitarian relief and its experience in helping countries move beyond conflict give it special abilities in this realm. It would also be sensible to retain a number of special missions in countries with acute technical needs in areas where the United States is well positioned to help.

As a result of this process, AID's $500 million annual administrative budget could be reduced to roughly $300 million. That would cover ex-

TABLE 5-3. *Evolution of the U.S. Agency for International Development*

Year	Number of bilateral assistance programs	Number of employees
1993	120	11,500
2000	75	8,000

Source: Hon J. Brian Atwood, administrator, U.S. Agency for International Development, "Testimony before the Senate Committee on Appropriations, Subcommittee on Foreign Operations, Export Financing and Related Programs," Washington, D.C., March 20, 1996.

penses for a strong planning team of perhaps 200 individuals, costing about $20 million a year and charged with devising development strategy worldwide; roughly one-half as many missions as exist now worldwide; and a staff to monitor the work of various nongovernmental and multilateral organizations. By the approach taken in this study, these gross savings are assumed to be put back into official development assistance in more productive programs.

Other Savings

In addition to major organizational reforms, U.S. policymakers should also reconsider several specific categories of aid they now provide. Two of the key issues are aid to Israel and Egypt and those parts of the P.L. 480 food program not specifically designed for emergency relief.

The P.L. 480 food aid program is not only a humanitarian relief mechanism, but also an outlet for surplus U.S. agricultural goods. The latter purpose should be rethought, for the P.L. 480 program neither makes a major difference in overall U.S. agricultural trade (funding less than 1 percent of the total) nor helps most countries receiving the assistance. Title II is given to needy countries that are suffering acute crises and is highly desirable on humanitarian grounds. But Title I can distort local agricultural markets in developing countries, flooding markets with U.S. food when surpluses exist in ways that tend to lower food prices and thereby discourage local food production. Farmers who would otherwise plant and then take food to market decide not to bother—or fail to earn enough proceeds from their harvest to recoup initial costs. This change would save nearly $300 million a year.

One might reduce the grant economic aid given to Israel and Egypt, provided that it can be done gradually and with the understanding if not active encouragement of the two countries at issue. This economy makes good sense on substantive grounds but would be a false economy if it led to a diplomatic row with fallout for the peace process.

Such cuts have already occurred to an extent as inflation has eroded the buying power of aid that has tended to stay constant in nominal terms. They might be accelerated in the economic support funds to roughly twice the U.S. inflation rate (that is, a nominal cut of about 3 percent a year). In this way, ESF for the two countries would be cut in half, but foreign military financing kept constant (at least in nominal terms); total aid flows to Israel and Egypt would remain more than $2 billion and $1.5 billion, respectively. Savings to the United States would be somewhat greater than $1 billion a year after five years.

Such reductions would seem to fit with the reform agenda of Israeli prime minister Benjamin Netanyahu.[19] In the case of Egypt, they would also accord with the strategy for greater aid selectivity outlined in chapters 3 and 4. As we argue there, large amounts of outside aid are unlikely to produce positive results in countries with poor or mediocre macroeconomic policies, so there is little reason to expect particularly good returns from existing economic aid to Egypt.

6

Conclusions

*T*HE UNITED STATES needs to adopt a new approach to development assistance for poorer countries, adequately fund that approach, and try to convince other bilateral donors as well as the multilateral financial institutions to support it as well.

To make a new aid strategy work, proponents of foreign assistance must acknowledge the need to combine soft hearts with tougher heads. Aid skeptics should acknowledge, for their part, that foreign assistance is not very expensive and not a significant contributor to the U.S. deficit, that it seeks to wrestle with some very difficult and important challenges facing the United States and the rest of the world, and that adequate resources should be devoted to it.

Budget Implications

Our calculations show that global development aid should increase to about $80 billion a year, from its current level of roughly $60 billion, and that the United States should for its part restore development aid from the 1997 level of $9 billion to the $12 billion average of recent decades or slightly more. Although such funding increases would clearly be significant, they are not nearly as large as some proponents of aid would like. For example, the official UN goal that industrialized countries provide 0.7 percent of their GDP to help the world's poorer countries seems excessive and without sound economic foundation. The goal that we espouse for U.S. international spending would do no more than restore U.S. official development assistance to its 1993 level of roughly 0.15 percent of U.S. GDP. Other donors' aid would return to their 1990 average level of around 0.35 percent of GDP.

Not only does the 0.7 percent goal seem unnecessary, but the implication of many critics of U.S. aid policy—that this country has a moral obligation to restore its aid levels to the OECD average—seems unreasonable. There might be good policy reasons for the United States to do so, but fair sharing of the burden is not one of them. The contribution of the United States military to international stability and security is so unrivaled and the importance of that stability so great for developing countries as well as industrialized states that it makes little sense to view foreign aid contributions in isolation.

Nevertheless, the recent and planned future actions of some U.S. foreign aid critics are unwise. Budget cutters trying to extract large economies from a development aid account that represents about one half of one percent of the U.S. federal budget may feel penny wise, but they are really pound foolish.

International affairs activities are very inexpensive relative to the stakes involved. The trade promoted, wars averted, and environmental damage alleviated have dollar values potentially in the trillions of dollars. International spending, by contrast, is done by the billions—units of measurement a thousand times smaller.

More international aid resources are now needed. The historical record and basic macroeconomic analysis suggest strongly that poor countries with good economic policies can benefit from more aid than they are now receiving. The lessons from the development of the East Asian "tigers" such as Taiwan and South Korea are that developing countries can productively absorb at least $50 per capita per year over a period of roughly one to two decades. Such approaches, if recipients are committed to reform, are the most likely to help countries "graduate" from aid rolls in a reasonable amount of time.

That aid money, coupled with recipients' own resources, can go into building roads and other transportation infrastructure, supporting national programs in education and health, and expanding the reach of utilities and communications services. It can also help cover transition costs related to reforms, such as through balance of payments support and social safety nets.

A second major area where added money could do a great deal of good is in efforts to help countries recover from conflict. Despite the substantial (and perhaps somewhat excessive) resources being devoted to high-profile efforts in places like Bosnia and the West Bank and Gaza, problems in other conflict zones such as Central Africa are left to fester—in large part for lack of funds. In the United States, more dollars for the flexible economic support fund (ESF) would help solve this problem, provided that the money was not earmarked but left available for pressing emergencies. Roughly half a billion additional ESF dollars a year would be ample.

Overall, restoring U.S. development aid to a level around $12 billion a year, measured in constant 1997 dollars, should be adequate for these purposes. The increase in annual spending would represent about 0.2 percent of the federal budget.

Even with this increase, international spending would be doing more than its fair share to achieve deficit reduction, principally because of reductions in cold-war related security aid. As a fraction of GDP, it would amount to about two-thirds of its 1980s' level.

At these budget levels, the United States would continue to rely on others to provide most of the world's aid. It would probably remain at the bottom of the OECD list of generosity as determined by the percent of GDP devoted to development assistance. But it would remain second among donors in absolute terms. Coupled with its global leadership role in other realms and with its expertise and credibility in foreign assistance matters, that U.S. aid level would allow the United States to retain major influence in donor circles.

As things stand, however, the lack of American enthusiasm for foreign aid has begun to catch on in other countries. Official development assistance worldwide, although still higher than typical levels of the 1980s (and of previous decades), fell off about 10 percent in real terms between 1994 and 1995. Total private capital flows to developing countries picked up by much more than aid fell, but the money went to a certain subset of those countries, doing little to ease the drop in official financing for the world's poorest countries.

Aid Selectivity

Aid skeptics do have concerns that should be addressed. Much development assistance today does little or nothing to achieve its primary goal of fostering sustainable macroeconomic growth in recipient countries. By allowing the recipients to muddle along, aid can reduce the impetus for needed reforms and make recipients' economic performance no better or even worse than it would have been in the absence of aid. For that two-thirds of global development aid focused primarily on economic development, a much different approach is needed.

For these reasons, expanded funding levels for development assistance should be provided only if donors are prepared to draw lessons from the first half-century of the development experience and adopt a much more selective approach to aid.

What does it mean to give aid more selectively? Donors should provide generous assistance to spur general economic growth and support countrywide programs in education and other areas only when the policy frameworks of the recipients are sound. About $40 billion a year of the global development aid budget of $60 billion is intended for such purposes. But roughly half of that $40 billion is provided to countries that have policy frameworks inconsistent with economic growth. This practice needs to be revamped.

Care should be taken in implementing a strategy of selectivity. Donors should be wary of cutting off aid in situations where reformist politicians are making genuine attempts to improve their country's economic policies, yet face strong internal resistance to doing so. Donors should also be sensitive to the implications of aid cutoffs in cases where countries totter on the verge of civil or financial collapse. But in most cases, they should sharply reduce aid to poor performers.

The remaining $20 billion in global development aid is for humanitarian relief and grass-roots programs to support basic human needs such as health care, family planning, and nutrition. Such programs are desirable wherever need exists, largely independent of countries' governments or economic systems. However, in cases where recipient governments are weak, corrupt, or otherwise unreliable, donors may need to maintain a strong presence on the ground to reduce the potential for abuse.

The countries still heavily reliant on aid today are for the most part mired in levels of poverty comparable to those they endured when large-scale aid efforts began decades ago. Their citizens' lives may have improved in some respects as a result of aid efforts, but they have generally made very little economic and institutional progress. The citizens in aid-giving countries, particularly the United States, seem increasingly aware of this poor record and are now reacting against it. Just as welfare as a way of life is out of vogue in U.S. domestic politics, so too is aid to countries that remain dependent for decades. A strategy of greater aid selectivity on the part of donors might also serve to help reestablish domestic political support for overseas assistance in this country.

Effective aid does not require imposition on the recipients of a particular development model; nor does it require micro-management of their economic policymaking. Indeed, there is increasing agreement that aid is currently burdened with too many rather than too few conditions. At the same time, there is widespread consensus about what constitutes a "good" policy framework. The key characteristics are relatively open trading regimes, realistic exchange rates, low budget deficits and low inflation rates, relatively small public sectors, and markets unencumbered by consumer and producer subsidies or other distortions. There is still a broad debate about more general development objectives and about what constitutes effective aid. But we know now that establishing and sustaining such a policy framework is necessary for growth and therefore for poverty reduction (although not necessarily sufficient to achieve the latter objective).

Growth is by no means the sole objective of aid. Yet it is difficult to advance broader development goals without it. The track record of the fast-growing economies in East Asia supports this view, as do the more recent experiences of countries ranging from Chile and Costa Rica to Mauritius and Botswana.

In our view, donors should generally focus on the potential for growth. They should be somewhat wary of trying to use aid to induce political reforms. Targeted assistance for specific political purposes such as supporting local human rights organizations and media is useful. But ambitious efforts to shape countries' politics by fine-tuning aid flows do not appear appropriate in most cases. They not only ask too much of aid, but assume more than is actually known about how developing countries can best achieve economic growth and political stability. Aid should, however, clearly be cut off in cases of egregious and widespread violations of human rights—on moral grounds and because extreme political repression is unlikely to permit achievement of aid's goals of economic and human advancement.

Consistent with a more selective and effective approach to aid is a restructuring of U.S. bilateral aid to emphasize strong programs and to change weak or counterproductive ones. For example, the P.L. 480 food aid program should be focused only on disaster relief (provided through its so-called Title II) and not on providing an outlet for excess U.S. agricultural goods in countries whose own farm sectors may be damaged by the resulting price distortions. Economic aid to Israel and Egypt should be reduced, perhaps by a total of up to a billion dollars a year—though gradually and only after consultation with the governments of those two states so as to minimize damage to the Mideast peace process.

The U.S. Agency for International Development, already substantially streamlined in recent years, might accelerate its streamlining. It could end its missions in most countries unless there is a very special technical or political reason for the U.S. government to be there. Many other donor organizations—in fact, probably too many for the good of most recipients—have global presence and make demands on recipient governments' time and energies. AID has many strengths, but it is no longer the pioneer or dominant player in development circles that it once was, and its basic approach should be reconsidered accordingly.

Aid and America's Role in the World

The decline of great-power competition does not mean that international issues have become less complicated, less important, or in the end less potentially dangerous. Those who claimed that the end of the cold war spelled the "end of history" could not have been more wrong. Given the size of world populations, the nature of modern technology, and the interdependence of civilizations, there will probably be at least as much history made in the twenty-first century as there was in the twentieth.

With wisdom and commitment, the United States can increase the odds that twenty-first- century history will include a minimal number of catastrophes and the greatest progress and human advancement possible. Doing so means staying militarily strong and economically healthy and engaged. It also means emphasizing foreign assistance, diplomacy, and other tools of international affairs that are increasingly subject to a malignant neglect.

Combined with other initiatives, a new approach to development assistance could also help restore a sense of purpose to a Western alliance system that, as the twenty-first century approaches, no longer has the clarity of moral direction or long-term strategic vision that made it perhaps history's most successful community of nations in the twentieth.

Notes

Chapter One

1. Report of the Task Force on Foreign Assistance to the Committee on Foreign Affairs, U.S. House of Representatives, House Document 101-32 (February 1989).

2. Oil remains an important commodity obtained abroad, but the economic significance of most other goods is quite modest. See, for example, Paul Krugman, *The Age of Diminished Expectations* (MIT Press, 1992), pp. 103–05.

3. For good documentation of the willingness of the American people to remain significantly involved in international activities of various sorts, including those designed to serve humanitarian purposes, see Steven Kull, "What the Public Knows That Washington Doesn't," *Foreign Policy*, no. 101 (Winter 1995–96), pp. 102–15.

4. Democracy by itself, though undoubtedly helpful, was probably not a sufficient glue for the alliance or guarantor of peace, despite the arguments of the contemporary "democratic peace" theory of international relations studies. That theory, though not without merit, has considerable difficulty in handling many major wars of the past two centuries: the War of 1812; the American Civil War; possibly World War I (some would argue that Germany was a democracy at that time); and even World War II (Hitler had come to power out of the Weimar Republic's democratic elections—and it seems only partial solace that he had formally ended Germany's status as a democracy before embarking on the most devastating war in human history). See Michael Doyle, "Liberalism and World Politics," *American Political Science Review*, vol. 80 (December 1986), pp. 1151–69; Christopher Layne, "Kant or Cant: The Myth of the Democratic Peace," *International Security*, vol. 19, no. 2 (Fall 1994), pp. 5–49; John M. Owen, "How Liberalism Produces Democratic Peace," in *International Security*, vol. 19, no. 2 (Fall 1994), pp. 87–125; and Richard H. Ullman, *Securing Europe* (Princeton University Press, 1991).

5. For a very good and concise summary of this theory of hegemonic stability, first articulated by Charles Kindleberger, see Robert Gilpin, *The Political Economy of International Relations* (Princeton University Press, 1987), pp. 86–92.

6. For a view influenced by the failure of the victorious powers of World War I to devise a comparable system for their era, see E.H. Carr, *The Twenty Years' Crisis, 1919–1939* (New York: Harper & Row, 1964), p. 169.

7. For a perspective on how the multilateral banks can help catalyze flows of private capital in countries that have begun to turn the corner toward sustained economic growth, see Jacques de Larosière, *Promoting Private Investment: The Role of Multilateral Development Banks* (Brookings, 1997).

Chapter Two

1. In its first two years, the Clinton administration sought to rewrite the 1961 foreign assistance act and redefine the above categories into six new ones: promoting sustainable development, building democracy, promoting peace, providing humanitarian assistance, promoting U.S. prosperity, and advancing diplomacy. Its effort did not ultimately produce a new bill. In the absence of official stature, these categories do not seem helpful enough to be worth using in this study. They are too broad to illuminate the international affairs budget at a meaningful policy level, so they are not used here further.

The first Clinton administration category is not unlike the first traditional category, without the humanitarian assistance pieces; building democracy includes aid to the former Soviet republics and the traditional foreign information efforts; promoting peace includes all assistance to the Middle East as well as U.S. contributions for UN peacekeeping; providing humanitarian assistance includes refugee aid, disaster aid, and part of the P.L. 480 program; promoting prosperity includes the export-import bank, Overseas Private Investment Corporation, and part of the P.L. 480 program; and advancing diplomacy includes operating costs for the State Department and the Agency for International Development as well as support for UN agencies.

2. Secretary of Defense William J. Perry, *Annual Report to the President and the Congress* (February 1995), pp. 39–40. Costs indicated in Secretary Perry's report for special U.S. military activities in Korea, near Cuba, and in southern Iraq, while relevant for traditional security purposes, are not counted in the above totals because they are not relevant to peace operations or humanitarian relief efforts per se.

3. See, for example, Casimir A. Yost and Mary Locke, *U.S. Foreign Affairs Resources: Budget Cuts and Consequences* (Washington, D.C.: Institute for the Study of Diplomacy, Georgetown University, 1996), p. 38.

4. Karen W. Arenson, "Donations to Charities Rose 11 Percent Last Year, Report Says," *New York Times,* May 23, 1996, p. A24; U.S. Agency for International Development, *Development and the National Interest* (1989); Organization for Economic Cooperation and Development, *Development Assistance Report 1995* (Paris: OECD, 1996), p. A14.

5. See Congressional Budget Office, *Enhancing U.S. Security through Foreign Aid* (April 1994), p. 80; Anne O. Krueger, *Economic Policies at Cross Purposes* (Brookings, 1993), p. 45.

6. John P. Lewis, "Overview," in John P. Lewis, ed., *Strengthening the Poor: What Have We Learned?* (Washington, D.C.: Overseas Development Council, 1988), pp. 3–26; Krueger, *Economic Policies at Cross Purposes*, pp. 19–35; Richard Jolly, "Poverty and Adjustment in the 1990s," in Lewis, *Strengthening the Poor*, pp. 163–69.

7. Development Assistance Committee, "Financial Flows to Developing Countries in 1995: Sharp Decline in Official Aid; Private Flows Rise," Organization for Economic Cooperation and Development, Paris, June 11, 1996, pp. 2, 10.

8. Krueger, *Economic Policies at Cross Purposes*, p. 104.

9. Executive Office of the President, *Budget of the United States Government, Fiscal Year 1997*, Appendix (Washington, D.C.: Government Printing Office, 1996), pp. 88–89.

10. Development Assistance Committee, *Development Assistance Report 1995*, p. A96.

11. Congressional Budget Office, *Enhancing U.S. Security through Foreign Aid* (April 1994), p. 80.

12. Thomas W. Lippman, "U.S. Loses Rank in Global Giving," *Washington Post*, June 18, 1996, p. A10.

13. Development Assistance Committee, "Financial Flows to Developing Countries," pp. 9, 12.

14. Ibid., pp. 7, 12.

15. Organization for Economic Cooperation and Development, *Development Assistance Report 1995*, various appendix tables including pp. A13–A14, A21–A22, A43–A44, A47, A58, A59–A60.

16. According to the OECD, U.S. nongovernmental organizations provide slightly more than the average in unofficial aid—roughly 0.04 percent of GDP in the 1993/1994 time frame, in contrast to an average of 0.03 percent. Germans and British provide 0.05 percent, French 0.02 percent, Japanese none of note above their official governmental contributions, and Norwegians 0.12 percent. This private U.S. aid, together with other non-ODA forms of official assistance, is enough to put the United States above Italy's aid contributions as a percent of GDP, but leaves it well behind all other OECD countries. See Development Assistance Committee, "Financial Flows to Developing Countries," p. 12.

17. United Nations Development Program, *Human Development Report 1994* (New York: Oxford University Press, 1994), p. 73.

18. World Bank, *World Development Report 1995* (New York: Oxford University Press, 1995), pp. 198–99; Development Assistance Committee, *Development Cooperation* (Paris: OECD, 1996), p. A58.

19. World Bank, *World Debt Tables,* vol. 1 (Washington, D.C.: World Bank, 1996), pp. 7–11.

20. World Bank, *World Development Report 1995,* p. 186.

21. Unfortunately, its approach lumps health care and education together with planning and public administration in the first category, "social programs and administrative infrastructure." It also leaves a great deal in the "other" category.

22. OECD, *Development Assistance Report 1995,* pp. A45–A46.

23. See for example, United Nations Development Program, *Human Development Report 1994* (New York: Oxford University Press, 1994), p. 165; World Bank, *World Development Report 1990* (New York: Oxford University Press, 1990), p. 198.

Chapter Three

1. See Joan M. Nelson with Stephanie J. Eglinton, *Encouraging Democracy: What Role for Conditioned Aid?* (Washington, D.C.: Overseas Development Council, 1992), pp. 1–4; Robert S. McNamara, *The Post–Cold War World and Its Implications for Military Expenditures in the Developing Countries* (Washington, D.C.: World Bank, 1991), p. 23; Nicole Ball, "Levers for Plowshares: Using Aid to Encourage Military Reform," *Arms Control Today* (November 1992), pp. 11–17.

2. For a review of the conditions that facilitate growth, see Alberto Alesina and Roberto Perotti, "The Political Economy of Growth: A Critical Survey of the Literature," *World Bank Economic Review,* vol. 8, no. 3 (1994), pp. 351–71. A recent study at the World Bank, meanwhile, found positive and causal links between the degree of civil liberties and the returns to investment on World Bank projects. See Jonathan Isham, Lant Pritchett, and Daniel Kaufmann, "Governance and the Returns to Investment: An Empirical Investigation," mimeo, Policy Research Department, The World Bank, Washington, D.C., September 1995.

3. Joan M. Nelson and Stephanie J. Eglinton, *Global Goals, Contentious Means: Issues of Multiple Aid Conditionality* (Washington, D.C.: Overseas Development Council, 1993), pp. 3–4; see also Carol Graham, "Economic Austerity and the Peruvian Crisis: The Social Costs of Autocracy," *SAIS Review* (Winter-Spring 1993), vol. 13, no. 1.

4. See Nelson and Eglinton, *Global Goals,* pp. 60–62.

5. For more discussion, see Amnesty International, *Amnesty International Report 1995* (London: Amnesty International, 1995); Human Rights Watch, *Human Rights Watch World Report 1996* (New York: Human Rights Watch, 1996); U.S. Department of State, *Country Reports on Human Rights Practices for 1995,* Senate Print 103-7 (Washington, D.C.: Government Printing Office, 1996).

6. On Albania, see Thomas Carothers, "In Albania, One for the Thugs," *Washington Post,* June 6, 1996, p. A29; for a similar assessment of the utility of aid in

serving noneconomic goals, see Nelson and Eglinton, *Global Goals*, pp. 3–4, 57–64, 69–70.

7. For detail on the many and changing objectives of aid, see Nelson and Eglinton, *Global Goals*.

8. This new conceptualization of aid is noted by Lant Pritchett and David Dollar of the World Bank in a 1996 research project proposal on aid effectiveness, being undertaken in the Policy Research Department of the World Bank.

9. The average number of conditions on World Bank loans, for example, increased from twelve in 1980–88 to seventeen in 1989–91. See Nelson and Eglinton, *Global Goals*.

10. World Bank, *World Development Report 1991* (New York: Oxford University Press, 1991), p. 48.

11. See, for example, Nelson and Eglinton, *Global Goals*; Paul Mosley, Jane Harrington, and John Toye, *Aid and Power: The World Bank and Policy-Based Lending* (London: Routledge, 1991); and World Bank, *Adjustment in Africa* (Washington, D.C.: 1994).

12. Craig Burnside and David Dollar, "Aid, Policies, and Growth" (Washington, D.C.: World Bank, 1996).

13. The levels of aid vary significantly among African countries, meanwhile, with Mozambique receiving 98 percent of GNP in aid, Tanzania 40 percent, Madagascar 17 percent, and Nigeria 1 percent. Nelson and Eglinton, *Global Goals*, p. 56. In 1995, official flows, of all kinds, accounted for more than 90 percent of net inflows, with 74 percent of those being grants and 24 percent being concessional loans. Sub-Saharan Africa is the largest recipient of official development assistance, with roughly $17 billion in 1995. See Tony Hawkins, "Foreign Debt: Crisis Worsens," *Financial Times*, May 20, 1996.

14. Mosley, Harrington, and Toye, *Aid and Power*.

15. Tony Killick, *A Reaction Too Far: Economic Theory and the Role of the State in Developing Countries* (London: Overseas Development Institute, 1989), cited in Mosley, Harrington, and Toye, *Aid and Power*.

16. Burnside and Dollar, "Aid, Policies, and Growth."

17. Good trade performance is defined as a favorable (that is, positive, or at least not greatly negative) balance of payments as well as growth in exports. See Mosley, Harrington, and Toye, *Aid and Power*, p. 204. They compared nineteen SAL recipients with nineteen nonrecipients during the 1980–86 period.

18. Ibid., p. 217.

19. Of the fifty-five countries, fourteen had prolonged, high inflation and nineteen never went above the 20 percent average. See Michael Bruno and William Easterly, "Inflation's Children: Tales of Crises that Beget Reforms," paper presented to the American Economics Association Annual Meetings, January 1996.

20. For a description of the important role of certain institutions in sustaining

growth, see Alex Cukierman, Steven B. Webb, and Bilin Neyapti, "Measuring the Independence of Central Banks and Its Effects on Policy Outcomes," *World Bank Economic Review*, September 1995. For the critical role of liberalization or open trading regimes, see Jeffrey Sachs and Andrew Warner, "Economic Reform and the Process of Global Integration," *Brookings Papers on Economic Activity 1995:1* (Brookings, 1995).

21. Bruno and Easterly, "Inflation's Children." Of the nineteen low-inflation countries, eleven were in the franc zone, where inflation has been kept artificially low by a unified exchange rate (CFA) fixed to the French franc and subsidized by substantial amounts of bilateral aid. The franc zone countries have performed poorly on the growth front over time and have correspondingly high average poverty levels.

22. See John H. Johnson and Sulaiman Wasty, "Borrower Ownership of Adjustment Programs and the Political Economy of Reform," World Bank Discussion Papers 199 (Washington, D.C., 1993).

23. Ibid.

24. For Poland, see Simon Johnson and Marzena Kowalska, "Poland: The Political Economy of Shock Therapy," in Stephan Haggard and Steven B. Webb, *Voting for Reform: Democracy, Political Liberalization, and Economic Adjustment* (New York: Oxford University Press/The World Bank, 1994); and for Chile, see Genaro Arriagada and Carol Graham, "Chile: Sustaining Adjustment During Democratic Transition" in the same volume.

25. The "grant" element of these loans varies according to the particular country's risk. While a particular interest rate might not be concessional for a low-risk country like Korea, which could obtain the loan at the same or lower rates on the market, the grant element for a high-risk country like Zambia would be much higher, as Zambia would have to pay much higher rates on the market. The World Bank's soft loan window, the International Development Association, meanwhile, is designed for the poorest countries and provides interest-free credit.

26. For example, a number of low- to middle-income countries owed considerable sums to the international financial institutions and needed to borrow more to service those debts.

27. Nelson and Eglinton, *Global Goals*, p. 44.

28. The World Bank's adjustment lending review (1988) cited in Mosley, Harrington, and Toye, *Aid and Power*.

29. Ibid., p. 67.

30. Nelson and Eglinton, *Global Goals*, p. 68.

31. In theory, conditionality could also be credible if enforcement were applied at random and by surprise, but such a practice seems unlikely to be adopted (at least consciously). Mosley, Harrington, and Toye, *Aid and Power*.

32. Sachs and Warner, "Economic Reform and the Process of Global Integration."

33. These 117 are drawn from the 135 countries in the Heston-Summers data series, excluding 18 where there were insufficient data. Ibid.

34. Ibid.

35. These exceptions were Cape Verde, China, Hungary, and Tunisia. All of these except China pursued statist development strategies that produced resulted in growth in the 1970s, but then financial crises in the 1980s. China, meanwhile, is unique in its size and pursued a "two-track" strategy, freeing most of the economy (the agrarian sector) to produce according to market principles, while the state continued to control most of the industrial sector. Ibid.

36. One comprehensive study on this issue is Robert Cassen, *Does Aid Work?* (Oxford: Clarendon Press, 1994.

37. Ibid.

38. Tony Hawkins, "Foreign Debt: Crisis Worsens," *Financial Times*, May 20, 1996.

39. Safety nets for poor or vulnerable groups are often necessary during the course of reform. Like economic policies in general, the most effective safety nets are those that have a strong domestic commitment in the form of human and financial investments. Yet, particularly in very poor countries, foreign financing can be critical in providing the additional resources necessary to achieve significant coverage. See Carol Graham, *Safety Nets, Politics, and the Poor: Transitions to Market Economies* (Brookings, 1994).

Chapter Four

1. Organization for Economic Cooperation and Development, *Development Assistance Report 1995* (Paris: OECD, 1996), pp. A43–A44; United Nations Development Program (UNDP), *Human Development Report 1994* (New York: Oxford University Press, 1994), p. 74.

2. For more information on these calculations, see Congressional Budget Office, *Enhancing U.S. Security through Foreign Aid* (April 1994), pp. 51–58; UNDP, *Human Development Report 1994*, pp. 77, 164–65, 182–83; World Bank, *World Development Report 1992: Development and the Environment* (New York: Oxford University Press, 1992), pp. 7, 26, 173; and James P. Grant, *The State of the World's Children 1994* (New York: Oxford University Press, 1993), pp. 11–19.

3. Nicolas van de Walle and Timothy A. Johnston, *Improving Aid: The Challenge to Donors and African Governments*, Policy Essay no. 21 (Washington, D.C.: Overseas Development Council, 1996), pp. 3–4.

4. For a similar view, see Jeffrey Sachs, "Growth in Africa," *Economist*, June 29th, 1996, p. 21.

5. Staffan Burenstam Linder, *The Pacific Century: Economic and Political Consequences of Asian-Pacific Dynamism* (Stanford, Calif.: Stanford University Press, 1986), pp. 8, 12.

6. Moreover, although followers of U.S. aid to the Middle East may have a different impression, on a global scale military aid is quite modest—roughly $5 billion a year, according to 1993 data, with the United States accounting for three-fourths of the total (and its security aid to Israel and Egypt representing the vast bulk of that). See UNDP, *Human Development Report 1994*, p. 53.

7. It also provided another $1 billion annually in military assistance, but for present purposes those funds can be ignored.

8. See Anne O. Krueger, *Economic Policies at Cross Purposes* (Washington, D.C.: Brookings, 1993), pp. 163–64; U.S. Agency for International Development, *U.S. Overseas Loans and Grants and Assistance from International Organizations: Obligations and Loan Authorizations, July 1, 1945-September 30, 1994*, pp. 130, 261; UNDP, *Human Development Report 1994*, p. 174.

9. See Agency for International Development, *U.S. Overseas Loans and Grants: Obligations and Loan Authorizations FY 1946-FY 1992*, vol. 3; U.S. AID, *U.S. Overseas Loans and Grants*, pp. 142, 264; Central Intelligence Agency, *The World Factbook 1995–1996* (Washington, D.C.: Brassey's, 1995), pp. 444–45; UNDP, *Human Development Report 1994*, p. 72.

10. U.S. Agency for International Development, *U.S. Overseas Loans and Grants and Assistance from International Organizations: Obligations and Loan Authorizations, July 1, 1945-September 30, 1994*, pp. 10, 226. For a view corroborating our position that aid to Africa is nearly adequate in its overall resource flows, especially given the difficulty recipient governments have in putting that aid to well-coordinated, effective, and enduring use, see van de Walle and Johnston, *Improving Aid*, p. 4.

11. World Bank, *World Development Report 1995* (New York: Oxford University Press, 1995), pp. 162–63.

12. World Bank, *Adjustment in Africa* (New York: Oxford University Press, 1994), pp. 32–33, 154–155; Krueger, *Economic Policies at Cross Purposes*, pp. 19–22; John M. Staatz and Carl K. Eicher, "Agricultural Development Ideas in Historical Perspective," in Eicher and Staatz, *Agricultural Development in the Third World* (Baltimore, Md.: Johns Hopkins University Press, 1984), pp. 4–7.

13. See Jeffrey Sachs, "Growth in Africa," *Economist*, June 29, 1996, p. 21; for general debt data, see World Bank, *World Debt Tables*, vol. 1 (Washington, D.C.: World Bank, 1996), pp. 208–17; for descriptions of the September 1996 Paris Club accord, see Patti Waldmeir, "Debt Relief for Poorest Nations Near Final Accord," *Financial Times*, September 30, 1996; and Patti Waldmeir and Robert Chote, "World Bank Agrees to Fund to Cut Poor Nations' Debt," *Financial Times*, October 1, 1996.

14. Net ODA figures do not account for all debt repayments because some repayments are for nonconcessional loans. For example, a country might have borrowed at near-market rates from the World Bank, but later become impoverished enough to qualify for loans from the (concessional) International Devel-

opment Association. Those latter loans, which count as ODA, might then have been used to repay the earlier nonconcessional loans. Since the non-concessional loans were not ODA, repaying them would not show up in the ODA ledger. So aid flows would, in a sense, appear to be greater than they really were.

15. Congressional Budget Office, *Enhancing U.S. Security through Foreign Aid* (April 1994), p. 80; Agency for International Development, *U.S. Overseas Loans and Grants and Assistance from International Organizations*, CONG-R-0105 (1992).

16. See Nicole Ball with Tammy Halevy, *Making Peace Work: The Role of the International Development Community* (Washington, D.C.: Overseas Development Council, 1996), p. 5.

17. See U.S. AID, West Bank and Gaza Mission, Fact Sheet, May 1996.

18. One reason for the typically poor return on large infrastructure projects is the failure of donors to incorporate the contributions and participation of potential beneficiaries. Several studies of World Bank infrastructure projects, notably water-related projects, find such participation critical to their success and sustainability. See Samuel Paul, "Does Voice Matter? For Public Accountability, Yes," Policy Research Working Paper no. 1388, The World Bank, Washington, D.C., December 1994; and Ritu Basu and Lant Pritchett, "The Determinants of the Magnitude and Effectiveness of Participation: Evidence from Rural Water Projects," World Bank, Washington, D.C., July 1994.

19. U.S. Agency for International Development, "FY 96 USG-Funded Economic Development and Humanitarian Assistance for Bosnia-Herzegovina," May 9, 1996.

20. World Bank, European Commission, and European Bank for Reconstruction and Development, "Bosnia and Herzegovina, the Priority Reconstruction and Recovery Program: The Challenges Ahead," Discussion Paper no. 2, April 2, 1996, pp. 1–11.

21. World Bank, *World Development Report 1992: Development and the Environment* (New York: Oxford University Press, 1992), p. 174.

22. Daniel C. Esty and Jamison Koehler, "Restructuring the Global Environment Facility," Policy Focus, Overseas Development Council, Washington, D.C., 1993, no. 1.

23. See Carol Graham, *Safety Nets, Politics, and the Poor* (Brookings, 1994), pp. 1–20; William A. Douglas, "Workers and Economic Adjustment," in Larry Diamond and Marc F. Plattner, *Economic Reform and Democracy* (Baltimore, Md.: Johns Hopkins University Press, 1995), p. 201; UNDP, *Human Development Report 1994*, p. 164.

Chapter Five

1. See World Bank, *World Development Report 1991* (New York: Oxford University Press, 1991), p. 157; World Bank, *Adjustment in Africa* (New York: Oxford

University Press, 1994), pp. 5, 140–41, 266–69.

2. World Bank, *World Development Report 1993* (New York: Oxford University Press, 1993), pp. 238–39, 276–77; World Bank, *Adjustment in Africa*, pp. 268–69.

3. See Jeffrey Sachs and Andrew Warner, "Economic Reform and the Process of Global Integration," *Brookings Papers on Economic Activity, 1995: 1* (Brookings, 1995).

4. Generally, countries experiencing severe warfare over this period are excluded from consideration because data is incomplete for most of them. Thus the sample does not focus heavily on countries that might have received large amounts of humanitarian aid without any plausible hope of benefiting macroeconomically from the assistance.

5. Calculations based on data in World Bank, *World Development Report 1995* (New York: Oxford University Press, 1995), pp. 162, 210; Development Assistance Committee, *Development Cooperation* (Paris: OECD), editions for 1982, 1986, 1989, 1992, 1995.

6. See for example, Dani Rodrik, "Why Is There Multilateral Lending?" Annual World Bank Conference on Development Economics, Washington, D.C., May 1–2, 1995, p. 21; Peter Boone, "The Impact of Foreign Aid on Savings and Growth," London School of Economics, June 1994, pp. 4–5.

7. See Joan M. Nelson and Stephanie J. Eglinton, *Global Goals, Contentious Means: Issues of Multiple Aid Conditionality* (Washington, D.C.: Overseas Development Council, 1993), p. 15.

8. Susan L. Woodward, *Balkan Tragedy* (Brookings, 1995), pp. 47–113; Wolfgang H. Reinicke, "Can International Financial Institutions Prevent Internal Violence?: The Sources of Ethno-National Conflict in Transitional Societies," in Abram Chayes and Antonia Handler Chayes, ed., *Preventing Conflict in the Post-Communist World* (Brookings, 1996), pp. 312–27; Michael S. Lund, *Preventing Violent Conflicts* (Washington, D.C.: U.S. Institute of Peace, 1996), p. 87.

9. Definitions of poor and extremely poor are based on purchasing power parity measures; expressed in 1997 dollars, the thresholds are roughly $500 and $350 per capita, respectively. See World Bank, *World Development Report 1990* (New York: Oxford University Press, 1990), pp. 2, 29; United Nations Development Program, *Human Development Report 1995* (New York: Oxford University Press, 1995), pp. 178–79.

10. See also Jacques de Larosière, *Promoting Private Investment: The Role of Multilateral Development Banks* (Brookings, 1997).

11. See World Bank, *World Development Report*, pp. 162–63, 220–21; Congressional Budget Office, *Enhancing U.S. Security through Foreign Aid* (1994), p. 89.

12. Development Assistance Committee, *Development Cooperation 1995*, p. A17.

13. See Nicolas van de Walle and Timothy A. Johnston, *Improving Aid: The Challenge to Donors and African Governments*, Policy Essay no. 21 (Washington, D.C.: Overseas Development Council, 1996), pp. 2–3.

14. Nicolas van de Walle and Timothy A. Johnston, *Improving Aid to Africa*

(Washington, D.C.: Overseas Development Council, 1996), pp. 102–03; Francis M. Deng and others, *Sovereignty as Responsibility* (Brookings, 1996), p. 109; Michael Maren, *The Road to Hell: The Ravaging Effects of Foreign Aid and International Charity* (Free Press, 1997).

15. John W. Sewell and others, *Challenges and Priorities in the 1990s: An Alternative U.S. International Affairs Budget, FY 1993* (Washington, D.C.: Overseas Development Council, 1992), pp. 43–46. For an intermediate option that would meld most AID missions into U.S. embassy offices, see Lawrence S. Eagleburger and Robert L. Barry, "Dollars and Sense Diplomacy," *Foreign Affairs*, vol. 75, no. 4 (July/August 1996), p. 5.

16. Van de Walle and Johnston, *Improving Aid to Africa*, p. 112.

17. General Accounting Office, *Foreign Assistance: Status of USAID's Reforms*, GAO/NSIAD-96-241BR (September 1996), p. 13.

18. Testimony of the Honorable J. Brian Atwood, administrator, U.S. Agency for International Development, before the Senate Committee on Appropriations, Subcommittee on Foreign Operations, Export Financing and Related Programs," March 20, 1996.

19. See for example, "Independent Israel?" *Wall Street Journal*, July 11, 1996, p. 14.

Index